William George McGuckin

Whist Nuggets

Being certain whistographs historical, critical and humorous. Vol. 1

William George McGuckin
Whist Nuggets
Being certain whistographs historical, critical and humorous. Vol. 1
ISBN/EAN: 9783337286002
Printed in Europe, USA, Canada, Australia, Japan
Cover: Foto ©ninafisch / pixelio.de

More available books at **www.hansebooks.com**

WHIST NUGGETS

BEING CERTAIN

WHISTOGRAPHS

HISTORICAL, CRITICAL, AND HUMOROUS

Selected and Arranged
by

WILLIAM G. McGUCKIN

NEW YORK AND LONDON
G. P. PUTNAM'S SONS
The Knickerbocker Press

Electrotyped, Printed, and Bound by
The Knickerbocker Press, New York
G. P. Putnam's Sons

CONTENTS.

	PAGE
INTRODUCTORY	vii
MODERN WHIST	1
London Quarterly Review, January, 1871	
WHIST AND WHIST-PLAYERS	33
Abraham Hayward, in *Fraser's Magazine*, April, 1869	
THE THIRTY-NINE ARTICLES OF WHIST	112
Richard Irving Dunbar	
RHYMING RULES, MNEMONIC MAXIMS, AND POCKET PRECEPTS	120
William Pole	
THE DUFFER'S WHIST MAXIMS	123
Cavendish's *Card Essays*	
WHIST, OR BUMBLEPUPPY	
ON THINGS IN GENERAL	130
PRACTICE OF BUMBLEPUPPY	132
THINKING	144
THE DOMESTIC RUBBER	150
Whist, or Bumblepuppy? by "Pembridge." —Roberts Bros.	

Contents

	PAGE
CARDS SPIRITUALIZED	153
Anon.	
MRS. BATTLE'S OPINIONS ON WHIST . .	158
Charles Lamb	
LADIES' WHIST	173
The Spectator, 1890	
WHISTOLOGY	183
All the Year Round, March 17, 1860	
WHIST AT OUR CLUB	203
Blackwood's Magazine, May, 1877	
A HAND AT CARDS	230
American Whist Illustrated, by G. W. P.—Houghton, Mifflin, & Co., 1890	
A WHIST PARTY	238
The Tailor-Made Girl, by Philip H. Welch—Chas. Scribner's Sons, 1888	
AT BOVOR—PLAY A GREAT GAME OF WHIST	244
Happy Thoughts, by F. C. Burnand—Roberts Bros.	
GOSSIP :	
I. EDWARD EVERETT AT THE COURT OF ST. JAMES	266
Geo. Wm. Curtis in "Editor's Easy Chair." *Harper's Monthly Magazine*, May 1876	
II. METTERNICH'S WHIST	271
Chamber's Journal, February 28, 1863	
III. LORD LYTTON AS A WHIST-PLAYER .	274
Serjeant Ballantine's *Experiences of a Barrister's Life*.	

Contents

	PAGE
IV. SOME LITERARY RECOLLECTIONS . .	276
James Payn. Harper & Bros. 1871	
V. ANECDOTES	281
Cavendish's *Card-Table Talk*	
VI. ADVANTAGE OF SKILL AT WHIST . .	284
Cavendish's *Card-Table Talk*	
SOME WHIST CHAT	289
R. A. Proctor—*Longman's Magazine*	

INTRODUCTORY.

IN presenting to the reader this little heap of *Whist Nuggets*, the Collector begs to interpose a word of introduction—to explain the purpose that has guided their selection, and to express his appreciation of the courtesy of the proprietors on whose lands they have been picked up.

The Editor has not had in mind the compilation of a text-book on the principles of the noble game. Nevertheless it is hoped that the student of the scientific side of whist will find much to interest him in the first three numbers. Where the first two pass from the history of primitive whist to a discussion of the latest development of play, they will be found already somewhat old-fashioned, although hardly more than twenty years have passed since they were written. What may be called the body of the game, however, remains substantially what Hoyle and Mathews developed, as is made plain by a comparison with the *Thirty-nine Articles of Whist*, the third number, which the courtesy of Mr. Richard Irving Dunbar, one of the most accomplished whist-players in Gotham, enables the Editor to include, and which is a codification of the rules of whist as played by Mr. Trist, of New Orleans, a player from whom the master, Cavendish himself, has not been ashamed to learn.

No collection of whistographs would be complete which did not include one from the inimitable author of *Bumblepuppy;* and, by the courtesy of "Pembridge" and of his publishers in the old world and in the new, the assiduous bumblepuppist will find here all the consolation of which he or she has never felt the need.

To the lovers of fun, whether whist-players or occasional bumblepuppists, the Editor confidently recommends the great game at Bovor, as described by Mr. Burnand, in his *Happy Thoughts;* and to the courteous editor of *Punch* and his publishers this Editor's thanks are rendered.

The quiet English humor of *Whist at Our Club* offers a striking contrast to the pungent wit of the extract from Philip H. Welch's *Tailor Made Girl*, included by the kind permission of Messrs. Charles Scribner's Sons, as well as to that of a *Hand at Cards*, taken from G. W. P.'s *American Whist Illustrated*, with the author's permission and that of Messrs. Houghton, Mifflin & Co.

To all these, as well as to Mr. George William Curtis and the Messrs. Harper & Brothers, the Editor gives due and grateful credit elsewhere.

After the manner of his mightier brethren, the Editor, as whist-player and whist-lover, disclaims all responsibility for the opinions hereinafter set forth; and his desire not to abate one jot or tittle of an author's right to ungarbled citation must be his apology to his gracious reader for the repetitions that will be discovered, as well as for the appearance and reappearance of that *castaneous* relic, Talleyrand's remark anent the sadness of a whistless old age.

The cards are cut and dealt.

Mesdames et messieurs, faites votre jeu.

WHIST NUGGETS.

MODERN WHIST.

THE game of whist, after two centuries of elaboration, has now become a favorite amusement in all ranks of society, and especially with persons of great intelligence and ability. Numerous societies have been established expressly for its practice, and at many of the West End clubs it is played daily, particularly in the afternoon, when the mental faculties are more active than in the evening. At these little gatherings may be seen men of high rank, sitting at the same tables with others eminent in literature, science, art, or the public service —all testifying, by the earnestness with which their attention is fixed on the game, to its great intellectual attractions. In the best private circles, too, and in domestic society generally, its high character is becoming better appreciated, although the style of play is still far from what it ought to be.

Whist is of English origin, but its popularity is not confined to this country. On the Continent it has become fully naturalized; the finest player that ever lived was a Frenchman, and the most elaborate works on whist are by foreign authors. It has, in fact, extended over the whole earth; there is not a spot where European civilization prevails, where whist is not practised and prized. A published collection of *Whist Studies* dates from the tropics; in the rigor of the North American winter whist forms the occupation of the frozen-up inhabitants for months together; and in the wilds of Australia the farmers play at whist for "sheep points, with a bullock on the rubber."

We need not hesitate to give a place in our pages to an intellectual occupation of such high and universal interest; and we propose, first, to offer a concise history of the game; next, to describe the chief characteristics of its most modern and improved form; and, lastly, to add a few remarks on whist playing.

The early history of whist is involved in some obscurity. It is not to be supposed that a game of this high character should have sprung at once perfect into being; it has been formed by gradual development from elements previously existing. As early as the beginning of the sixteenth century a card-game was in common use, of which both the name and the chief feature enter prominently into the construction of whist. This was called *triumph*—corrupted into *trump*—and the essence of it was the predominance of one particular suit, called the triumph or trump-suit, over all the others. It was of Continental origin, like most of the card games in use at that period. A work published in Italy in 1526 speaks of it under the name of *Trionfi*, and it is mentioned by Rabelais as *la Triumphe*, among the games played by Gargantua. From France it was imported into England, where it soon became popular in good society, as we find a reference to it in a quarter where it would hardly be looked for, namely, in a sermon preached by Latimer at Cambridge the Sunday before Christmas, 1529. He mentions the game under its corrupted as well as its original appellation, and clearly alludes to its characteristic feature, as the following extracts will show:

"And where you are wont to celebrate Christmass in playing at cards, I intend by God's grace to deal unto you Christ's Cards, wherein you shall perceive Christ's Rule. The game that we play at shall be called the Triumph, which, if it be well played at, he that dealeth shall win; the Players shall likewise win; and the standers and lookers upon shall do the same.

* * * * * *

"You must mark also that the Triumph must apply to fetch home unto him all the other cards, whatever suit they be of.

* * * * * *

"Then further we must say to ourselves, What requireth Christ of a Christian man? Now turn up your Trump, your Heart (Hearts is Trump, as I said before), and cast your Trump, your Heart, on this card."

Other references to this game are found at a later period; we need only mention two. In *Gammer Gurton's Needle*, said to be the first piece performed in England under the name of a comedy, and written by Bishop Still soon after the middle of the sixteenth century, occurs this passage :

> " *Chat.* What, Diccon? come nere, ye be no stranger:
> We be set fast at trump, man, hard by the fyre.
> Thou shalt set on the king, if thou come a little nyer.
>
> * * * * * *
>
> Come hither, Dol ; Dol, sit downe and play this game,
> And, as thou sawest me do, see thou do even the same :
> There is five trumps besides the queene, the hindmost thou shalt find her ;
> Take hede of Sim Glover's wife, she hath an eie behind her."

Another reference is by Shakespeare. In *Antony and Cleopatra,* act iv., scene 12. Antony says :

> " My good knave, Eros, now thy Captain is
> Even such a body : here I am Antony ;
> Yet cannot hold this visible shape, my knave.
> I made these wars for Egypt ; and the Queen,—
> Whose heart I thought I had, for she had mine ;
> Which, whilst it was mine, had annex'd unto 't
> A million more, now lost,—she, Eros, has
> Pack'd cards with Cæsar, and false played my glory
> Unto an enemy's *triumph.*"

This passage has been the subject of several comments ; but the repeated allusions to card-playing leave no doubt as to the reference in the last word.

The game of Triumph appears to have been played in several different ways, some of which resembled our present *Écarté*; they had, however, little similarity to whist, except in the feature of the predominance of the trump-suit, which was common to them all.

About the beginning of the seventeenth century the game had acquired in England another name, which is also preserved in whist, namely *Ruffe*. It has often excited curiosity how the word for an ornament to the neck or wrists should have come to be used for this purpose; but it is possible it may have been only another corruption of the original French *triomphe*, as there is much similarity in the sounds. At any rate the terms were synonymous, as Cotgrave, in his *French and English Dictionary*, 1611, explains the French word *triomphe* to mean "the card-game called ruffe or trump"; and Nares in his Glossary says "ruff meant a trump card, *charta dominatrix*."

But contemporaneously with this change,

the game itself had also undergone, in England, some modifications which caused it to differ materially from the original foreign type, and among these was the attachment of certain advantages, or "honors," to the four highest cards of the trump-suit. This was probably of itself an ancient invention, for we find a game called "*Les Honeurs*" in Rabelais' list; but the importation of it into trump, or ruff, gave the game a new character, and it took the name of "Ruff-and-honors," the original form being called "French ruff" for distinction.

Ruff-and-honors was played with a pack of fifty-two cards, the ace ranking the highest. There were four players, two being partners against the other two, and each received twelve cards; the remaining four were left as a stock on the table, and the top one was turned up to determine the trump-suit. The player who happened to hold the ace of trumps had the privilege of taking the stock in exchange for four cards of his own, an operation called *ruffing*. The score was nine, and the partners that won most tricks were "most forward to win the set." Three honors in the joint hands were reckoned equivalent to two tricks, and four honors to four. This came very near to whist, and was, in fact, whist in an imperfect form.

The further changes in the constitution of the game, and the radical alteration of the name, appear to have taken place early in the seventeenth century. The first form of the new designation was *Whisk*, a word which occurs in *Taylor's Motto*, by Taylor, the Water Poet, published in 1621. Speaking of the prodigal, he says:

" He flings his money free with carelessnesse,
 At novum, mumchance, mischance (chuse ye which),
 At one-and-thirty, or at poore-and-rich,
 Ruffe, slam, trump, nody, whisk, hole, sant, new cut."

The origin of the word is obscure; but, in default of a better explanation, it has been suggested that it was used by the common people as a synonym for *ruff*, in ridicule of the affectations of the gallants who played at the game. The article of dress in fashion under the latter name at the time is described as

"great and monsterous, made either of cambric, holland, lawne, or els of some other the finest cloth that can be got for money, whereof some be a quarter of a yard deepe, yea some more, hanging over their shoulder-points, instead of a vaile. But if Æolus with his blasts, or Neptune with his storms, chaunce to hit upon the crasie barke of their bruised ruffles, then they goeth flip-flap in the winde, like ragges that flew abroad, lying on their shoulders like the disheclout of a slut."

This sort of thing might well be ridiculed as a *whisk*, which not only meant "a small besom or brush," but also referred to an article of dress :

> " Their wrinkled necks were covered o'er
> With whisks of lawn, by grannums wore
> In base contempt of bishops' sleeves."

Thirty or forty years after Taylor's mention of the word, as applied to the game, it had become changed to its present form, the earliest known use of which is quoted by Johnson from the second part of *Hudibras* (spurious), published in 1663:

> " But what was this? A game at Whist,
> Unto our Plowden-Canonist."

In 1674 we find a published description of the game in a curious book, ascribed to Charles Cotton the poet, and entitled *The Compleat*

Gamester; or Instructions how to play at Billiards, Trucks, Bowls, and Chess; together with all manner of usual and most gentile Games, either on Cards or Dice.* In this book a chapter is devoted to "English Ruff-and-Honors and Whist," and it contains the following passage:

"Ruff-and-honours (*alias* slamm) and Whist, are games so commonly known in England, in all parts thereof, that every child almost of eight years old hath a competent knowledge in that recreation."

After describing ruff-and-honors the author says, "Whist is a game not much differing from this." The ruffing privilege was abolished; each player still had twelve cards, but, instead of leaving an unknown stock on the

---

* The frontispiece to this book represents various games being played, and is accompanied by a punning description of them in verse. One figure shows a game at whist, in which ladies take part, and the rhyme says:

"Lastly observe the women with what grace
They sit and look their partners in the face,
Who from their eyes shoot Cupid's fiery darts,
Thus make them lose at once their game and hearts.

    *   *   *   *   *   *

Ladies don't trust your secrets in that hand
Who can't their own (to their own grief) command,
For this, I will assure you, if you do,
In time you 'll lose your Ruff and Honour too."

table, the four deuces were discarded from the pack before dealing; a great step in advance, as it enabled the players to calculate with more certainty the contents of each other's hands. The score was still nine, tricks and honors counting as before.

Cotton never uses or alludes to the earlier name "*whisk*," but he gives an independent derivation of the newer word. He says the game

"is called whist from the silence that is to be observed in the play."

This meaning is warranted by the custom of the time. The word, although treated as a verb, adjective, or participle by Shakespeare, Milton, Spenser, and others, is defined by Skinner (1671), one of the best authorities, as *interjectio silentium imperans;* and so it was commonly used. In an old play, written by Dekkar in 1604, we find the example:

"Whist! whist! my master."

Cotton's derivation of the present name has been adopted by Johnson and Nares, and has always been most commonly received; but it must not be forgotten that the word "*whisk*" is the older of the two, and that it continued in use, along with the other name, for a century after Cotton wrote. Pope, in his epistle to Mrs. Teresa Blount, 1715, says:

" Some squire, perhaps, you take delight to rack,
  Whose game is Whisk, whose treat a toast in sack."

Johnson describes whist as "vulgarly pronounced whisk"; and the Hon. Daines Barrington, writing, in 1786, on games at cards, adopts the later orthography without any qualification.

It is possible to reconcile the two derivations by supposing that, when the game took its complete form, the more intellectual character it assumed demanded greater care and closer attention in the play; this was incompatible with noise in the room or with conversation between the players, and hence the word "*whist!*" may have been used in its interjectional form to insist on the necessary silence; and from the similarity of this to the term already in use the modification in the last letter may have taken its rise. It is worthy of remark, that in a fashionable book on *Ombre*, published in Berlin in 1714, the writer, who had probably never heard of the English game, says : "*Pour bien jouer l'ombre, il faut du silence et de la tranquillité.*"

But, whatever may be the views held in this country as to the origin of the name of our national card-game, it is only fair to our ingenious neighbors across the Channel to give their explanation, which we find in a French work on whist :

"At a time when French was the current language in England, the people had become so infatuated with one of their games at cards, that it was prohibited after a certain hour. But parties met clandestinely to practise it ; and when the question " *Voulez-vous jouer ?* " was answered by " *Oui !* " the master of the room added the interjection "*St !*" to impose silence. This occurred so often that " *Oui-st* " became at length the current appellation of the game ! "

With these names there came to be associated another of a very strange character, namely "*swabbers*" or "*swobbers*." Fielding, for example, in the account of Jonathan Wild's visit to the sponging-house in London, in 1682, says, "whisk and swabbers was the game then in the chief vogue." Swift, in his *Essay on the Fates of Clergymen*, ridicules Archbishop Tenison, who was said to be a dull man, for misunderstanding the term. He relates a well-known story of a clergyman, who was recommended to the Archbishop for preferment, when his Grace said, "He had heard that the clergyman used to play at *whist and swobbers;* that as to playing now and then a sober game at whist for pastime, it might be pardoned; but he could not digest those wicked *swobbers.*" "It was with some pains," adds the Dean, "that my Lord Somers could undeceive him." Johnson quotes the pretended speech of the Archbishop, and defines *swabbers* as "four privileged cards, which are only incidentally used for betting at whist." These were probably identical with the four honors; and it has been conjectured that as "*whisk*" was intended to ridicule "*ruff,*" the analogous term "*swabbers*" (from swab, a kind of mop) may have been added to supply the place of the other part of the original name; so that "*whisk and swabbers*" was made the vulgar synonym for the "*ruff and honors*" of the fashionable world. But, however this may be, the additional term was of limited application, and soon went out of use.

It is curious that although the precursors of whist had enjoyed favor in high places, yet whist itself, in its infancy, was chiefly played in low society, where cheats and sharpers assembled. The greatest part of Cotton's chapter is devoted to a warning against the tricks and frauds of these gentry. He alludes to the "arts used in dealing," and shows how, by ingenious devices, "cunning fellows about this city may not only know all the cards by their backs, but may turn up honors for themselves, and avoid doing so for their adversaries." The following passage gives some significant hints:

"He that can by craft overlook his adversaries' game hath a great advantage, for by that means he may partly know what to play securely. There is a way to discover to their partners what honours they have; as by the wink of one eye, or putting one finger on the nose or table, it signifies one honour; shutting both the eyes, two; placing three fingers or four on the table, three or four honours."

In a republication of Cotton's work in 1734,

these cautions are amplified, showing that whist still retained the same low character. The editor says, "as whisk [he uses the old appellation] is a tavern game, the sharpers generally take care to put about the bottle before the game begins." A special chapter is given to "piping at whisk"; and as this is an accomplishment not generally known at the modern clubs, the following extract may be interesting:

"By piping I mean when one of the company that does not play (which frequently happens), sits down in a convenient place to smoke a pipe and so look on, pretending to amuse himself that way. Now the disposing of his fingers on the pipe, while smoking, discovers the principal cards that are in the person's hand he overlooks, which was always esteemed a sufficient advantage to win a game. This may also be done by another way, *i.e.*, without the pipe, and by common conversation. 'Indeed,' signifies diamonds; 'truly,' hearts; 'upon my word,' clubs; 'I assure you,' spades." *

It is only fair to add, that with the bane the editor supplies also the antidote. He says,

* "There are several other bare-faced practices made use of, such as looking over hands, changing cards under the table, and often from off the table; but these are generally made use of by women, who, when detected, laugh it off, without any sense of shame or dishonour."— *Annals of Gaming.*

"*For which reasons, all nice gamesters play behind curtains.*"

There is other evidence of the low character of whist. In Farquhar's comedy of the *Beaux's Stratagem*, 1707, Mrs. Sullen speaks of "the rural accomplishment of drinking fat ale, playing at whisk, and smoking tobacco with my husband." Fielding and Pope, as we have seen, both speak of it disparagingly ; and Thomson, in his *Autumn* (1730), describes how, after a heavy hunt dinner,

> "Whist awhile
> Walks his dull round beneath a cloud of smoke
> Wreath'd fragant from the pipe."

This being, he adds, one of the "puling idlenesses" introduced to cheat the thirsty moments until the party

> " Close in firm circle, and set, ardent, in,
> For serious drinking."

In the early part of the eighteenth century there was a mania for card-playing in all parts of Europe and in all classes of society, but in the best circles whist was still unknown. Gentlemen in their gaming coteries chiefly practised piquet (a very old game, invented in France in the fifteenth century), and in ladies' society the most fashionable amusement was *Ombre*, immortalized by Pope's *Rape of the Lock* (1712), in a manner strongly contrasted with his disparaging mention of whist a year or two later.

It was about 1730 when the new game rose out of its obscurity and took rapidly the rank due to its great merits. At that time the ordinaries, where gambling had been long carried on to an enormous extent, and with the most scandalous abuses, began to be superseded by the more intellectual meetings at taverns and coffee-houses, which figure so prominently in the literary annals of the last century. It happened that a party of gentlemen who frequented the Crown coffee-house in Bedford Row, and of whom the first Lord Folkstone was one, had become acquainted with the game, and practised it at their meetings. They soon found out it had merits, studied it carefully, and arrived, for the first time, at some fundamental rules of play.

The way having been thus prepared, there was wanting a man of genius who should further work out the elements of the game, and mould it into a permanent, logical, scientific form. This man appeared in the person of EDMOND HOYLE. There is very little trustworthy information as to his antecedents. He was born in 1672 : it is said he studied as a barrister, and he styles himself in his first book " a gentleman." It is clear he was a man of good education, and moved in good society ; probably he was one of the party that met at the Crown.

It appears that he had studied whist for many years ; and he saw, not only that it had great capabilities, but that it was much debased by the use made of it by sharpers for cheating inexperienced players out of their money. He believed that it was in his power to guard the public against these unprincipled practices, as well as to excite a more legitimate interest in the game, by spreading a better knowledge of the principles on which it should be played ; and to attain these objects he resolved to teach it professionally. His spirited attempt excited much attention, as we find several notices of it on record. In the *Rambler* of May 8, 1750, a lady writes :

"As for play, I do think I may, indeed, indulge in that, now I am my own mistress. Papa made me drudge at whist till I was tired of it; and, far from wanting a head, Mr. Hoyle, when he had not given me above forty lessons, said I was one of his best scholars."

In the *Gentleman's Magazine* of February, 1755, a writer, professing to give the autobiography of a fashionable physician, says :

"Hoyle tutored me in several games of cards, and, under the name of guarding me from being cheated, insensibly gave me a taste for sharping."

In the course of this instruction he sold to his pupils a set of notes which he had drawn up, containing rules and directions for their guidance. These were in manuscript, and he charged a guinea for each copy. The novelty and great value of the rules were soon discovered, and surreptitious copies began to get into circulation, when Mr. Hoyle to secure his copyright, had them published.

At this time the final changes had been made by increasing the score to ten, and by using the whole pack, thus giving thirteen cards to each player. This latter improvement introduced the *odd trick*, an element of such great interest in the present game. Whether it was Hoyle or some one previously, who made these changes, is not clear; but at any rate the game, as he presents it, is precisely the form of long whist ever since played.

His book had a great and rapid success; it went through several editions in one year, and it seems to have been again pirated, as the author found it necessary to certify every genuine copy by attaching his autograph signature, of which the following, taken from the thirteenth edition is a fac-simile.

Edmond Hoyle

In the fifteenth edition the signature was, for the first time, impressed from a wood-block, and in the seventeenth it was announced that, "Mr. Hoyle was dead." The great man departed this life, full of years and of honors, on the 29th of August, 1769.

Byron's oft-quoted parallel—

"Troy owes to Homer what whist owes to Hoyle,"

hardly does justice to our author, for he was far more than the historian of whist; he may, essentially, be considered its founder.

The effect of Hoyle's promulgation of the game in its improved form was very prompt, as we learn from a witty and amusing brochure that appeared in the same year, 1743, called *The Humours of Whist, a dramatic Satire, as acted every day at White's and other Coffee-houses and Assemblies*. It is a short comedy, the principal characters being Professor Whiston (Hoyle), who gives lessons in the game; Sir Calculation Puzzle, an enthusiastic player, who muddles his head with Hoyle's calculations and always loses; pupils, sharpers, and their dupes. The object is chiefly to ridicule the pretensions of Hoyle and the enthusiasm of his followers, and to show that skill and calculation are of no avail against bad luck or premeditated fraud. The work was reprinted ten years later, but it is scarce, and we may give a few extracts that throw light on the circumstances attending the first introduction of the new rules of the game.

Hoyle had given out that he had spent forty years in its study, and the prologue says :

> " Who will believe that man could e'er exist,
> Who spent near half an age in studying whist ?
> Grew grey with calculation, labour hard,
> As if life's business center'd in a card ?
> That such there is, let me to those appeal
> Who with such liberal hands reward his zeal.
> Lo ! whist he makes a science, and our peers
> Deign to turn schoolboys in their riper years."

Sir Calculation Puzzle gives some amusing explanations of his losses. In one case he says :

> " That certainly was the most out-of-the-way bite ever was heard of. Upon the pinch of the game, when he must infallibly have lost it, the dog ate the losing card, by which means we dealt again, and faith he won the game."

Again, in reference to Hoyle's calculations of chances :

> " We were nine all. The adversary had three and we four tricks. All the trumps were out. I had queen and two small clubs, with the lead. Let me see : it was about

222 and 3 halves to—'gad, I forgot how many—that my partner had the ace and king; ay, that he had not both of them, 17 to 2; and that he had not one, or both, or neither, some 25 to 32. So I, according to the judgment of the game, led a club; my partner takes it with the king. Then it was exactly 481 for us to 222 for them. He returns the same suit, I win it with my queen, and return it again; but the devil take that Lurchum, by passing his ace twice, he took the trick, and, having two more clubs and a thirteenth card, egad, all was over."

The praise of Hoyle's book by its supporters is unbounded. They say:

"There never was so excellent a book printed. I'm quite in raptures with it; I will eat with it, sleep with it, go to Parliament with it, go to Church with it. I pronounce it the gospel of whist-players. I want words to express the author, and can look on him in no other light than as a second Newton. I have joined twelve companies in the Mall, and eleven of them were talking of it. It's the subject of all conversation, and has had the honour to be introduced into the Cabinet."

The wits, however, did not neglect to poke fun at the Professor:

"*Beau.* Ha! ha! ha! I shall dye! Yonder is Lord Finess and Sir George Tenace, two first-rate players; they have been most lavishly beat by a couple of 'prentices. Ha! ha! ha! They came slap four by honours upon them almost every deal.

"*Lord Rally.* I find, Professor, your book do's not teach how to beat four by honours. Ha! ha! ha!

"*Professor* [aside]. Curse them! I'd rather have given a thousand pounds than this should have happen'd. It strikes at the reputation of my Treatise.

"*Lord Rally.* In my opinion there is still something wanting to compleat the system of whist: and that is A Dissertation on the Lucky Chair. [*Company laugh.*]

"*Professor.* Ha! ha! ha! your Lordship's hint is excellent. I'm obliged to you for it."

Whist advanced rapidly in public favor, and evidence is on record of the time when it was received at court and formally acknowledged as one of the royal amusements. In 1720 a little book called the *Court Gamester* was, as its title-page informs us, "written for the use of the young princesses," the daughters of the Prince of Wales, afterwards George II. It was frequently reprinted, and in later editions a second part was added, called the *City Gamester*, containing less polite games used east of Temple Bar. Whist was included in the latter category up to the seventh edition; but in the next, dated 1754, it was transferred to the court division. In 1758 it had become a fit recreation for University dons, as in No. 33 of the *Idler*, the senior fellow of a college at Cambridge represents himself and his party as "sitting late at whist in the evening."

When whist became fashionable it was naturally taken up by polite literature, dry rules and laws being made subservient to poetry and imagination. We have already seen how it had been dramatized; it was now to be raised to a higher grade in Parnassus, by becoming the subject of an epic. In 1791 appeared *Whist, a Poem, in 12 Cantos*, by Alexander Thomson, Esq. The book went through two editions, and made great pretensions to learning, by quotations from or references to authors in almost every language, from French to Persian, and of almost every age, from the Patriarchs to the eighteenth century; but the poetry was feeble, the history incorrect, and the whist not over sound. One quotation, of the concluding lines, will suffice:

> " Nor do I yet despair to see the day
> When hostile armies, rang'd in neat array,
> Instead of fighting, shall engage in play:
> When peaceful whist the quarrel shall decide,
> And Christian blood be spilt on neither side.
> Then pleas no more should wait the tardy laws,

> But one odd trick at once conclude the cause.
> (Tho' some will say that this is nothing new,
> For here there have been long *odd tricks* enow).
> Then Britain still, to all the world's surprise,
> In this great science shall progressive rise,
> Till ages hence, when all of each degree
> Shall play the game as well as Hoyle or me."

One of the chief seats of whist-playing during the eighteenth century was the city of Bath, where Nash and other celebrities had much encouraged card-games generally. About 1800 a little book appeared there, entitled *Advice to the Young Whist Player*, by Thomas Matthews, Esq. This was a sound and useful work, containing many improvements, resulting from the experience of half a century, and it is, even now, worthy of attentive study.

About the same date an important change took place, namely, the introduction of "Short Whist," by altering the winning score from ten to five, and abolishing the "call" for honors when wanting two of game. The change is said to have originated in an accident: Lord Peterborough having one night lost a large sum of money, the friends with whom he was playing proposed to give him the *revanche* at five points instead of ten, in order to afford him a quicker chance of recovering his loss. The new plan was found so lively that it soon became popular, and has long since superseded long whist in the best circles. The reason of the preference is not difficult to discover. All good players must have found out how the interest increased towards the close of the long game, when the parties were pretty even, and when it became necessary to pay stricter attention to the score, in order to regulate the play. Now to cause this state of things to recur more frequently, it would be sufficient to play, as it were, the latter half of the game without the former, *i. e.*, *to commence with both parties at the score of five;* for this is the true sense of the alteration.

This mode of viewing it accounts for no change being made in the value of the honors. Some authorities think the scoring for these should have been halved, and, no doubt, this would have given more effect to skill in play; but such a change would have rendered the game less generally interesting. It must never be forgotten that the element of chance is one of the attractive features of whist, to good players as well as to mediocre ones, and to tamper with the present arrangement would probably endanger the popularity of the game.

Whist was known in France at an early period by translations of Hoyle. It was played by Louis XV., and under the Empire was a favorite game of Josephine and Marie Louise. After the Restoration it was taken up more enthusiastically. "The nobles," says a French writer, "had gone to England to learn to think, and they brought back the thinking game with them." Talleyrand was the great player of the day, and his *mot*—"You do not know whist, young man? What a sad old age you are preparing for yourself!"—is a standing quotation in all whist books. Charles X. was playing whist at St. Cloud on the 29th of July, 1830, when the tricolor was waving on the Tuileries, and he had lost his throne. His successor, Louis Philippe, when similarly engaged, had to submit to an elegant insolence.

He had dropped a louis, and stopped the game to look for it, when a foreign ambassador, one of the party, set fire to a billet of 1,000 francs to give light to the King under the table.

In 1839 appeared a *Traité du Whiste*, by M. Deschapelles, whom Mr. Clay calls "the finest whist player, beyond any comparison, the world has ever seen." Much was to be expected from such a quarter, but the publication was but a fragment of a larger work that never appeared. The author treats of whist in a manner highly *spirituel*. He reasons on immensity and eternity, on metaphysical necessity and trial by jury; he invokes the sun of Joshua and the star of the Magi; he investigates the electrical affinities of the players, and illustrates a hand by analytical geometry. He died some fifteen or twenty years ago.

The latest stage in the history of whist comprises the more modern determination and consolidation of its scientific constitution, both theoretical and practical.

This important step was brought about by a circumstance somewhat similar to that which gave rise to the first development of the game by Hoyle, a century and a quarter before. Between 1850 and 1860 a knot of young men at Cambridge, of considerable ability, who had at first taken up whist for amusement, found it offer such a field for intellectual study, that they continued its practice more systematically, with a view to its complete scientific investigation. Since the general adoption of short whist the constant practice of adepts had led to the introduction of many improvements in detail, but nothing had been done to reduce the modern play into a systematic form, or to lay it clearly before the public; its secrets, so far as they differed from the precepts of Hoyle and Matthews, were confined to small coteries of club players. The little whist school held together afterwards in London, and added to its numbers; and in 1862 one of its members brought out the work published under the name of "Cavendish," the principal object of which was to illustrate the modern play by a set of model games, after the manner of those so much used at chess. Two years afterwards appeared the essay of Mr. Clay, and a little later that of Dr. Pole.

Each of these publications is distinct in its object. The work of Dr. Pole expounds the fundamental theory on which the modern game is based; that of Cavendish gives detailed rules for, and examples of, its application in practice; and that of Mr. Clay is an able dissertation on the more refined points of the best modern play, by the best modern player. Taken together, these books (which ought to be combined in one volume) furnish a complete epitome of the game, presenting it both theoretically and practically in the perfect state at which it has now arrived, by continued study and practice during the two centuries that have elapsed since it first assumed a definite shape and took its present name.

London Quarterly Review.

WHIST AND WHIST-PLAYERS.

THE laws of whist, like those of Nature before Newton, lay hid in night, at all events were involved in most perplexing confusion and uncertainty, when the happy thought of fixing, defining, arranging and (so to speak) codifying them, occurred to a gentleman possessing the requisite amount of knowledge and experience, and admirably qualified by social position for the task. "Some years ago," writes Mr. Baldwin in May, 1864, "I suggested to the late Hon. George Anson (one of the most accomplished whist-players of his day) that, as the supremacy of short whist was an acknowledged fact, a revision and reformation of Hoyle's rules would confer a boon on whist-players generally, and on those especially to whom disputes and doubtful points were constantly referred. Our views coincided, but the project was, for the following reason, abandoned."

The reason was neither more nor less than what has stopped or indefinitely postponed so many other projects for the amelioration of society or improvement of mankind, namely, the difficulty and trouble to be encountered, with a very uncertain chance of success. This reason was eventually outweighed by the sense of responsibility in the face of a steadily increasing evil which a decided effort might correct; and early in 1863 the legislator of the whist-table had duly meditated his scheme and made up his mind as to the right method of executing it. When Napoleon had resolved upon a code, he began by nominating a board of the most eminent French jurists, whose sittings he was in the constant habit of attending, and by whom it was, article by article, settled and discussed. Mr. Baldwin proceeded in much the same fashion. The board or committee which met at his suggestion, or (as he says) "kindly consented to co-operate with him," was comprised

of seven members of the Arlington Club, who—
we might take for granted, were it not notorious
as a fact—were renowned for the skilful practice
as well as the scientific knowledge of the game.

The foundation of the republic of Venice
may be dated from 697 A.D., when twelve of the
founders met and elected the first Doge. Their
descendants, *gli Elettorali*, formed the first
class of the aristocracy, and with them were
subsequently associated the descendants of the
four who joined in signing an instrument for
the foundation of the Abbey of San Giorgio
Maggiore. The twelve were popularly spoken
of as the Twelve Apostles, and the four as the
Four Evangelists. The foundation of the republic of whist may be dated from its reduction
under settled laws; and precedence such as was
accorded to the Venetian Apostles and Evangelists should be accorded to the two bodies of
gentlemen by whom Mr. Baldwin's suggestions
were so effectively carried out. The seven
members of the Arlington (who may rank with
the Apostles) were:—George Bentinck, Esq.,
late M. P. for West Norfolk; John Bushe, Esq.

(son of the Chief Justice in "Patronage"); John Clay, Esq., M. P., who acted as chairman; the late Charles C. Greville, Esq.; Sir Rainald Knightley, Bart., M. P.; H. B. Mayne, Esq.; G. Payne, Esq.; Colonel Pipon. The Resolution appointing them is authenticated by the distinguished signature of Admiral Rous. The code drawn up by them was transmitted to the Portland Club, the whist-club *par éminence* since the dissolution of Graham's, which nominated the following committee (who may rank with the Evangelists of Venice) to consider it :—H. D. Jones, Esq. (the father of "Cavendish"), chairman; Charles Adams, Esq.; W. F. Baring, Esq.; H. Fitzroy, Esq.; Samuel Petrie, Esq.; H. M. Riddell, Esq.; R. Wheble, Esq. Their suggestions and additions were immediately accepted by the Arlington, and on Saturday, April 30, 1864,—it is right to be particular—this resolution was proposed and carried unanimously:

"Arlington Club.
"That the Laws of Short Whist as framed by the Whist Committee, and edited by John Loraine Baldwin, Esq., be adopted by this Club.
"(Signed) Beaufort, Chairman."

So soon as this resolution was passed, the work was done; for all the other principal clubs in town and country eagerly notified their adhesion, and it would be simply absurd for individuals to refuse obedience. That the Continent and the New World will do well to follow the lead of England, may be inferred from a single point of comparison. Mr. Baldwin's *Laws of Whist* are comprised in sixteen pages, whereas two hundred and eighty-four pages of M. Deschapelles' *Traité du Whist* are devoted to the laws. Nor is the code the only boon for which we are indebted to the codifier. He has also been the means of eliciting what (when it was first published) was incomparably the acutest, most compact, and most practical essay on the subject, *A Treatise on the Game*, by J. C. (John Clay). It was preceded by several works of merit, but its improving effects may be traced in all recent editions of the best; and we have now a literature of whist which leaves the habitually bad player, male or female, without the semblance of an apology.

Although the large circulation of these books would imply general study and corresponding advance, the effect has been disappointing upon the whole. It is quite curious to see how many who have made whist their favorite occupation never rise to the rank of third-rate players; how many are utterly ignorant of the plainest principles, and unprepared for the most ordinary combinations or contingencies; how many are almost always in hopeless confusion about their leads; how many have not the smallest notion why and when they should trump a doubtful card, or why and when they should lead trumps. The Italian who had the honor of teaching George III. the violin, on being asked by his royal pupil what progress he was making, observed, "Please your Majesty, there are three classes of players: 1. Those who cannot play at all. 2. Those who play badly. 3. Those who play well. Your Majesty is just rising into the second class." This is the outside compliment we could pay to a numerous section of assiduous whist-players. Yet, as Lord Chesterfield told his son, whatever is worth doing at all is worth doing well; and one would have thought that a few hours' study might be advantageously bestowed in escaping this constantly recurring condition of embarrassment, to say nothing of the annoyance which may be read in the partner's face, however indulgent or well bred, when he or she happens to know something of the game.

This want of proper grounding and training, far from being confined to the idle and superficial, is frequently detected or avowed in the higher orders of intellect, in the most acute, accomplished, and cultivated minds. "Lady Donegal and I," writes Miss Berry, "played whist with Lord Ellenborough and Lord Erskine. I doubt which of the four plays worst." Lord Thurlow declared late in life that he would give half his fortune to play well. Why did he not set about it? Lord Lyndhurst and Lord Wensleydale were on a par with Lord Ellenborough and Lord Erskine, yet they were both very fond of the game, and both would eagerly have confirmed the justice of Talleyrand's well-known remark to the youngster who rather boastingly declared his ignorance of it: "*Quelle triste vieillesse vous vous préparez!*" * It is an invaluable resource to men of studious habits, whose eyes and mental faculties equally require relief in the evening of life or after the grave labors of the day; and the interest rises with the growing consciousness of skill.

The main cause of this educational omission or neglect is the rooted belief that whist cannot be taught by study or reading, which is pretty nearly tantamount to saying that it cannot be taught at all; for there was no reason why a sound precept, orally communicated at a card-table should be less sound and useful when printed in a book. Moreover, the book has one marked advantage over the oral instructor: it gives time for reflection, and does not give occasion for irritability. We have no elementary schools of whist nor paid teachers as in

---

* To Talleyrand at the whist-table might be applied, with the change of a word, the couplet of Pope:

"See how the world its veterans rewards,
A youth of plotting, an old age of cards."

Talleyrand was far from a good player, and, as might have been anticipated, unduly prone to finessing and false cards.

billiards; and a competent amateur, when taking his place opposite a lady partner, is almost invariably addressed : " Now pray don't scold ; I can't bear scolding." In other words : " I can't bear to be taught." Even when a lady requests to be told if she plays wrong, the odds are that, unless she is resolutely bent on fascinating, she will turn upon you, if you are simple enough to take her at her word, like the matron in *Cœlebs* who was lamenting her own exceeding sinfulness :

"*Mr. Ranby :* You accuse yourself too heavily, my dear ; you have sins to be sure.
"*Mrs. Ranby* (in a raised voice and angry tone): And pray what sins have I, Mr. Ranby ? "

A critical remark to a male partner, or an attempt to talk over the hand, is frequently met in a manner that does not invite a repetition of the experiment, although a polite inquiry why a particular card was played is an implied compliment. Mr. Clay speaks with his characteristic good sense on this topic :

"Talking over the hand after it has been played is not uncommonly called a bad habit, and an annoyance. I am firmly persuaded that it is among the readiest ways of learning whist, and I advise beginners, when they have not understood their partner's play, or when they think that the hand might have been differently played with a better result, to ask for information, and invite discussion. They will, of course, select for this purpose a player of recognised skill, and will have little difficulty in distinguishing the dispassionate and reasoning man from him who judges by results, and finds fault only because things have gone wrong. They will rarely find a real whist-player so discourteous as to refuse every information in his power, for he takes interest in the beginner who is anxious to improve."

But real whist-players will rarely take sufficient interest in beginners, however anxious to improve, to be willing to cut in with them before a certain amount of progress has been made; and a request for information, betraying a want of elementary knowledge might provoke an answer like Dr. Johnson's to the young gentleman who asked him whether the cat was oviparous or viviparous : "Sir, you should read the common books of natural history, and not come to a man of a certain age and some attainments to ask whether the cat lays eggs." With reference, also, to your own immediate interest, you had better hold your tongue, or reserve your comments till the party has broken up; for the offender will immediately play worse.

Books, therefore, are the readiest and surest sources of instruction, but to begin with books would be as absurd as the practice of teaching Latin and Greek through the medium of a Latin grammar. It is now admitted that the Hamiltonian method of learning languages is the best. Acquire a sufficient stock of words before meddling with syntax. Just so, familiarize yourself with the ordinary combinations of the cards before venturing on the rules and principles which constitute the syntax of the game. But in each case the syntax is indispensable, when the appropriate stage of progress has been reached; and the whist-player who endeavors to dispense with it, unless he is singularly gifted, will bear the same relation to one of the master spirits of the Portland, the Arlington, or the Paris Jockey Club, that a courier or quick-witted lady's maid who had made the tour of Europe, would bear in linguistic acquirements to the trained diplomatist who speaks and writes

French, German, and Italian with correctness and facility.

It is the same in all things to which mind can be applied; theory or science should go hand in hand with practice. This is true even of games of manual dexterity, like billiards and croquet, but it is pre-eminently true of whist. Nay, we shall show before concluding that the mere mechanical quality of memory has far less to do with making a fine or even a good player, than the higher qualities of judgment, observation, logical intuition, and sagacity.

The introduction of short whist is thus described by Mr. Clay:

"Some eighty years back, Lord Peterborough having one night lost a large sum of money, the friends with whom he was playing proposed to make the game five points instead of ten, in order to give the loser a chance, at a quicker game, of recovering his loss. The late Mr. Hoare, of Bath, a very good whist-player, and without a superior at piquet, was one of this party, and has more than once told me the story."

Major A, writing in 1835, says: "Short whist started up and overthrew the ancient Long Dynasty more than half a century ago," thus confirming Mr. Clay as to the date; but if it started up in the eighteenth century, its supremacy was not established till far into the nineteenth, and many whist-players now living imbibed their rudiments under the ancient Long Dynasty.

An illustration in the *Anti-Jacobin* of 1798, goes far to prove that long whist alone was present to the minds of the distinguished writers, Mr. Canning and Mr. Frere:

> " Of whist or cribbage mark th' amusing game,
> The partners changing, but the sport the same ;
> Else would the gamester's anxious ardour cool,
> Dull every deal, and stagnant every pool.
> —Yet must *one* Man, with one unceasing Wife,
> Play the Long Rubber of connubial life."*

These high authorities differ as to the origin. " This revolution," continues Major A., " was occasioned by a worthy Welsh baronet preferring his lobster for supper hot. Four first-rate

*The *Progress of Man*, a parody on Mr. Payne Knight's *Progress of Civil Society*, in which a marked preference is given to the connubial rites or ceremonies of the South Sea Islands over those of Great Britain. This is alluded to in the preceding lines of the parody :

"Learn hence, each nymph, whose free aspiring mind,
Europe's cold laws and colder customs bind—
Oh ! learn what Nature's genial laws decree,
What Otaheite is, let Britain be."

whist-players—consequently, four great men—adjourned from the House of Commons to Brookes's, and proposed a rubber while the cook was busy. 'The lobster must be hot,' said the baronet. 'A rubber may last an hour,' said another, 'and the lobster be cold again, or spoiled, before we have finished.' 'It is too long,' said a third. 'Let us cut it shorter,' said a fourth.—Carried, *nem. con.* Down they sat, and found it very lively to win or lose so much quicker. Besides furnishing conversation at supper, the thing was new—they were legislators, and had a fine opportunity to exercise their calling."

Next day (he says) St. James' Street was in commotion: the Longs and Shorts contended like the Blues and Greens of the circus: and for a period it was regarded as a drawn battle or a tolerably equal contest: but the old school became gradually weaker by deaths, and the new school, when no longer confronted by habit and prejudice, obtained a complete victory. The truth is, the new game is the better of the two, as requiring more sustained attention, more rapidity of conception, more dash, more *élan*, and giving more scope to genius than the old. It is the Napoleonic strategy or tactics against the Austrian; or (to borrow an illustration from naval warfare) it may be compared to Nelson's favorite manœuvre of "breaking the line." Those who maintain the contrary, must maintain that the second half of the old game (when it stood five to five) was less critical and less calculated for the display of skill than the first. At all events the popular decree is irrevocable, and the revolution has been rendered more complete by circumstances which are appositely stated by Mr. Clay:

"I remember, as a youngster, being told by one of the highest authorities, on the occasion of my having led a single trump from a hand of great strength in all the other suits, that the only justification for leading a singleton in trumps was the holding at least ace and king in the three remaining suits. He spoke the opinion of his school. That school, I am inclined to believe, might teach us much that we have neglected, but I should pick out of it one man alone, the celebrated Major Aubrey, as likely to be very formidable among the best players of the present day. He was a player of great original genius, and refused strict adherence to the over careful system, to which his companions were slaves.

"But whist had travelled, and thirty or more years ago we began to hear of the great Paris whist-players. They sometimes came among us—more frequently our champions encountered them on their own ground, and returned to us with a system modified, if not improved, by their French experience. . . . We were forced to recognize a wide difference between their system and our own, and 'the French game' became the scorn and the horror of the old school, which went gradually to its grave, with an unchanged faith, and in the firm belief that the invaders, with their rash trump leading, were all mad, and that their great master, Deschapelles—the finest whist-player beyond any comparison the world has ever seen—was a dangerous lunatic. The new school, however, as I well remember, were found to be winning players."

Now what are the distinctive features of the new school, its essential principles, its merits, and its defects? Unluckily, the great master, Deschapelles, did not live to carry out his original plan. He has left only a single chapter on *La Doctrine*, entitled, *De l'Impasse* (Of the Finesse). But his mantle has fallen on no unworthy successors, and little difficulty will be experienced in rendering his system intelligible to those who care to master it, for it is substantially that which all the best players in both hemispheres have adopted and recommend:

"The basis of the theory of the modern scientific game of whist [says Professor Pole] lies in the relations existing between the players.

"It is a fundamental feature of the construction of the game, that the four players are intended to act, not singly and independently, but in a double combination, two of them being *partners* against a partnership of the other two. And it is the full recognition of this fact, carried out into all the ramifications of the play, which characterizes the scientific game, and gives it its superiority over all others.

"Yet, obvious as this fact is, it is astonishing how imperfectly it is appreciated among players generally. Some ignore the partnership altogether, except in the mere division of the stakes, neither caring to help their partners or be helped by them, but playing as if each had to fight his battle alone. Others will go farther, giving *some* degree of consideration to the partner, but still always making their own hand the chief object; and among this latter class are often found players of much skill and judgment, and who pass for great adepts in the game."

The combined principle was not ignored, it was simply undervalued, by the old school. What they failed to see, and what many modern players cannot be brought to see yet, is that, with tolerably equal cards, the result of the mimic campaign hangs upon it, as the fate of Germany hung on the junction of Prince Charles and the Crown Prince at Sadowa, or the fate of Europe on the junction of Blucher and Wellington at Waterloo. Of course it is necessary to agree upon a common object or system, and this again is placed in the clearest light by Professor Pole:

"The object of play is of course to make tricks, and tricks may be made in four different ways, viz.:

"1. By the natural predominance of *master cards*, as aces and kings. This forms the leading idea of beginners, whose notions of trick-making do not usually extend beyond the high cards they have happened to receive.

"2. Tricks may be also made by taking advantage of the *position* of the cards, so as to evade the higher ones, and make smaller ones win : as, for example, in finessing, and in leading up to a weak suit. This method is one which, although always kept well in view by good players, is yet only of accidental occurrence, and therefore does not enter into our present discussion of the general systems of treating the hand.

"3. Another mode of trick-making is by *trumping;* a system almost as fascinating to beginners as the realization of master cards ; but the correction of this predilection requires much deeper study.

"4. The fourth method of making tricks is by establishing and bringing in a *long suit*, every card of which will then make a trick, whatever be its value. This method, though the most scientific, is the least obvious, and therefore is the least practised by young players.

"Now the first, third, and fourth methods of making tricks, may be said to constitute different *systems*, according to either of which a player may view his hand and regulate his play."

This is illustrated by an example. The hand of the player with whom the opening lead lies is thus composed: *Hearts* (trumps), queen, nine, six, three. *Spades*, king, knave, eight, four, three, two. *Diamonds*, ace, king. *Clubs*, a singleton. He may lead off the ace and king of diamonds (System No. 1), or the singleton in the hope of a ruff (No. 3), or the smallest of his long suit (No. 4), on the chance of establishing it and making three or four tricks in it. In other words, he has to choose between the three systems; and the paramount importance of the choice consists in its deciding the opening lead, by far the most important of the whole; as it is the first indication afforded to the partner. "He will, if he is a good player, observe with great attention the card you lead, and will at once draw inferences from it that may perhaps influence the whole of his plans."

When the highest authorities, on the most careful calculation of chances, have laid down that the long-suit system is the best, and the long-suit opening has become the received method of carrying it out, a player who takes his own line, or looks exclusively to his own hand, will wilfully commit what Mr. Clay justly calls "the greatest fault he knows in a whist-player." All that can be said in favor of the rival systems has been said a hundred times and deliberately set aside, but the strongest of all objections to each of them is, that neither admits of combined action, in fact, can hardly be called a system at all; for when you have led off your ace and king, you are at a standstill, and when you have led your singleton, you have probably embarrassed instead of informing your partner; and it is fortunate if you have not led him into a scrape. Besides, you may have no ace and king, and no singleton; whereas you must always have what (comparatively speaking) may be called your strong suit, if only consisting of four.

Players who find an irresistible fascination in leading their best cards, or in trumping, may also take comfort in the reflection that they are not requested to abandon their favorite tactics altogether; for occasions are constantly arising when it becomes advisable to fall back upon them; just as the most consummate general may be compelled to resort to defensive or guerilla warfare, when he is too weak to hazard a pitched battle or a siege in form. It can hardly ever be right to lead off an ace and king with no other of the suit, for they are almost sure of making at a more opportune period of the game. But when held with others in an otherwise weak hand, *i. e.*, without strength in trumps, or the chance of establishing a suit, high cards may be judiciously led at once to avoid being trumped. Whenever, therefore, a good player plays out his winning cards, without first playing trumps, it is a manifest token of weakness, instead of an exhibition of strength.

The argument is thus summed up by Professor Pole:

" Accepting, therefore, this system as the preferable one, we are now able to enunciate the fundamental theory of the modern scientific game, which is:

" *That the hands of the two partners shall not be played singly and independently, but shall be combined, and treated as one. And that in order to carry out most effectually this principle of combination, each partner shall adopt the long-suit system as the general basis of his play.*"

Mark the words "general basis." This is quite enough to bring about the required understanding, and you are at full liberty to adapt your play to circumstances when your partner makes no distinct call upon you, or is unable to co-operate in the execution of a plan.

It is an obvious corollary that the primary use of trumps is to draw the adversary's trumps for the purpose of bringing in your own or your partner's long suit; and it is consequently essential to determine what strength in trumps justifies you in leading them. There is a capital sketch of a whist party in *Sans Merci*, by the author of *Guy Livingston*, in which the hero, who is losing to a startling amount, asks his partner, an old hand, whether with knave five he ought not to have led trumps. "It has been computed," was the calm reply, "that eleven thousand Englishmen, once heirs to fair fortunes, are wandering about the Continent, in a state of utter destitution, because they would not lead trumps with five and an honor in their hands." Professor Pole is distinct and positive on this point:

"Whenever you have five trumps, *whatever they are*, or whatever the other components of your hand, you should lead them; for the probability is that three, or at most four, rounds will exhaust those of the adversaries, and you will still have one or two left to bring in your own or your partner's long suits, and to stop those of the enemy. * * * And, further, you must recollect that it is no argument against leading trumps from five, that you have no long suit, and that your hand is otherwise weak; for it is the essence of the combined principle that you work for your partner as well as yourself, and the probability is that if you are weak, *he* is strong, and will have long suits or good cards to bring in. And if, unfortunately, it should happen that you are both weak, any other play would be probably still worse for you."

Cavendish says that, with the original lead and five trumps, you should almost always lead one; with six, invariably. Colonel Blyth, after giving the same qualified opinion in his text, adds in a note: "I once heard a first-rate whist-player say that, with four trumps in your hand, it was mostly right to lead them; but that he who held five, and did not lead them, was fit only for a lunatic asylum." This first-rate whist-player had probably recently been playing with one of the eleven thousand, or with strong-minded females who are most provokingly reticent of trumps. We should recommend every incipient whist-player, who has not experience enough to mark the rare exceptional cases, to lead one when he holds more than four, but to pause and reflect with four. With four small trumps, he should not lead one, unless he is strong in all the other suits, or at least strong enough in each to prevent the establishment of an adversary's strong suit. If there are two or more honors amongst his four, or the ace, he may lead one with comparatively little risk.

The smallest should be led from four or more, except when you lead from a sequence, or except when you have king, knave, ten, with others, when the received lead is the ten. Mr. Clay has laid down *nem. con.* (at least, *nem. con.* amongst the authorities) that with ace, king, and others in trumps, you should lead the lowest, unless you have more than six, *i. e.*, as an original lead, or before circumstances have called for two rounds certain. The reason is that you may otherwise lose the third and most important trick; for if you have no more than six, the odds are that one of your adversaries has at least three, headed by a superior card to your third best. The odds are also in favor of your partner holding the queen or knave, and if the queen is on his right, the knave is commonly as good as the queen. With ace, king, knave, and three small trumps, it may be as well to lead the ace and king, on the chance of the queen falling. With ace, king, knave, and less than three, the approved practice is to lead the king, and wait for the return of the lead to finesse the knave.

With a hand requiring or justifying a trump lead, the fact of an honor being turned up on your right must be disregarded, even with a certainty of its taking your partner's best card, the grand object being to get the command of trumps, not the first trick in them. Unless you wish the lead in trumps to be returned, do not (at least not early in the hand) lead through an honor, for the practice of leading through honors, except as a regular trump lead, has been fortunately given up. We say fortunately, for, so long as it prevailed, it was impossible to know whether the lead through the honor was the regular lead of trumps or not. At the same time, an experienced player may exercise his discretion in refraining from immediately returning the lead up to a high honor, especially if he can replace the lead in his partner's hand, and so enable him to lead through the honor a second time.

There is another case when you may avoid returning a lead of trumps, whether through an honor or not, *i. e.*, when your partner has evidently led from weakness or desperation in a peculiar condition of the game. Thus, when he leads a knave, you may take for granted that it is his best, for (in England) there is no recognized trump lead from knave with a higher in the hand. The lead of the ten may be from king, knave, ten, with or without others, and may place you in doubt unless you know that your partner cannot have both king and knave. In our opinion you should always, when third player, pass the ten of trumps unless you see your way clear to winning both that and the two following tricks. If it does not make, it forces an honor and compels your left-hand adversary to play up to you. It is quite painful to see an ace or king put upon a ten evidently led from weakness, and the command of trumps thus irrecoverably lost. The time for this lead is when the game is obviously lost, or in great jeopardy, unless your partner is strong in trumps. For example, your adversaries are three love, and your only trump, or highest of two or three, is the ten. The game is lost unless your partner has two honors, and your ten will materially strengthen him, if he has.*

The same state of things may justify or require a trump lead, even when you have no trump that can be called strengthening, not even a nine; but the lead of a singleton in trumps at the commencement of the game, with nothing in the state of the score to justify it, strikes us to be reprehensible in the extreme. We do not go the length of saying with the champion of the old school, quoted by Mr.

---

* On the same principle, when, to enable you to save the game, it is necessary that the remaining cards should be placed in a particular manner, play as if you knew them to be so placed. This is the secret of many of the most celebrated instances of fine play.

Clay, that the only justification for leading a singleton in trumps (presumably not an honor) is holding at least ace and king in the three remaining suits. But there should be strength in each of the three remaining suits sufficient to prevent the establishment of a long suit by the adversaries. There is also this essential objection: The first duty of a player is to decide, after a careful study of his cards, whether he is to play a superior or inferior part, whether he is to be commander or subordinate for the hand, whether he is to act on the offensive or defensive, to aim at winning or saving the game. Now, with one trump and no great strength in other suits, you have no right to assume the command by forcing a trump lead on your partner, who, with a single honor and without what can be called strength in trumps, may manage to save the game, if you do not force him into the sacrifice of his best card at starting. Leave him to initiate the lead of the trumps either by leading or asking for them. Begin with your high cards and watch for the signal; if it is not forthcoming, go on with them and force. If you have no high cards, *cadit questio:* you would be clearly wrong to lead the trump.

As for people who lead trumps because they are at a loss what else to lead, they might just as well take the most important step in life, go into orders, the army, or Mrs. Starr's convent, marry, or get unmarried, from sheer lassitude and vacuity. It is Lord Derby's leap in the dark repeated on a small scale. A trump lead almost always brings matters to a crisis, and should never be hazarded without reason. If absolutely no semblance of a reason suggests itself, play any card rather than a trump; and if this blank state of mind is of frequent recurrence after a resolute effort to improve, we should address the dubitant pretty nearly as the French fencing-master addressed the late Earl of E. at the conclusion of six months' teaching : "Milord, je vous conseille decidemment d'abandonner les armes."

The importance of the trump lead can hardly be over-estimated when we consider that (with the exceptions already hinted at) it should be returned immediately. It is an aphorism of traditional respectability that the only excuses for not returning a trump are a fit of apoplexy or not having any.* These, too, are the only available excuses for not leading trumps, when your partner *asks* for them, and leading them in a manner to carry out his supposed wishes to the full.

* The following case fell under our own observation: A. (the leader) had ace, king, two small spades (trumps); tierce major, two other clubs; two diamonds and two hearts. B. (left-hand adversary), queen, three small trumps; tierce major and two other diamonds, three hearts, one club. C. (A.'s partner), knave and one small trump; ace, king, long suit of hearts; diamonds and one club. D., three trumps, one heart; diamonds, and clubs. B. and D. were three love. A. led a trump which was won with the knave by C., who (instead of returning the lead) led hearts, which were trumped the second round by D.; who then led a diamond and established a kind of sea-saw, B. winning with diamonds, and D. trumping hearts. To stop this, A. over-trumped with his king, and led his ace of trumps; leaving B. with the queen and another. B. trumped the second lead of clubs, drew the remaining trumps, made his remaining diamonds, and won the game. If C. had returned the trump, he and his partner *must* have won the game, and *might* easily have made every trick but one; for, after three rounds of trumps, A. would have forced the queen, re-established his suit with his remaining trump, and then, instructed by his partner's discards of diamonds, have led hearts. From the moment the second lead of hearts began there was, demonstrably, no manner of play by which he could save the game, much less win it. C.'s excuse for not returning the trump was that *she* (it is commonly a fair amateur who reasons in this fashion) kept it to trump her partner's strong suit, clubs. Playing out high cards before returning the trump is incurring the very risk the trump lead is intended to obviate.

"It [asking for trumps] consists in *throwing away an unnecessarily high card*, and it is requisite to pay great attention to this definition. Thus, if you have the deuce and three of a suit of which two rounds are played, by playing the three to the first round and the deuce to the second, you have signified to your partner your wish that he should lead a trump as soon as he gets the lead. The same with any other higher card played *unnecessarily* before a lower."

Mr. Clay, after a satisfactory defence of its fairness, goes on to contend that this signal should never be given simply because the demandant would rather have trumps played upon the whole. He regards it as tantamount to saying: "I am so strong that, if you have anything to assist me, I answer for the game, or, at least, for a great score. Throw all your strength into my hand, abandon your own game, at least lead me a trump, and leave the rest to me."

So grave does the resulting responsibility appear to this master of the art, that, he tells us, it is not in his recollection that he ever took this liberty with his partner when he held less than four trumps, two honors, or five trumps, one honor, along with cards in his or (obviously) in his partner's hand which made the fall of the trumps very plainly advantageous, adding: "I am far from saying, that with the strength in trumps which I have described, it is always, or even generally, advisable to ask for trumps. I have only ventured to lay down that which, in my opinion, should be the minimum."

Upon this conventional understanding, a partner with two or three trumps should lead the best, and if it makes, follow with the next best: with ace, queen, and another, lead the ace, then the queen, and then the other, unless checked by an indication that either adversary has no more. With four, unless headed by the ace, lead the lowest, with an ace and others, the ace. Keeping in view the main object, the strengthening of your partner, no player of ordinary sagacity can be at a loss how to meet a call for trumps.

In returning a lead, whether in plain suits or trumps, if you have not decided strength, you should be guided by the same principle of self-sacrifice. Having only three originally, you should return the best; with four or more originally, the lowest. Thus, with ace, ten, three, and deuce, you should win with the ace, and return the deuce. With ace, ten, and deuce only, you win with the ace and return the ten. This not only strengthens your partner; it enables him to count your hand:

"In trumps, for instance, when he holds one, with only one other left against him, he will very frequently know, as surely as if he looked into your hand, whether that other trump is held by you, or by an adversary. It follows from the above that you should not fail to remark the card in your own lead, which your partner returns to you, and whether that which he plays to the third round is higher or lower than that which he returned."

The principle is partially applicable to original leads. Thus, if you have only two or three cards of a suit with nothing higher than a knave, lead the highest: if you are compelled to lead from ace, king, or queen, and a small one, lead the highest; and it is occasionally right with queen and two small ones, to lead the queen, thereby giving your partner the option of passing it, and at all events strengthening him where you are weak.

The safest leads are from sequences; and the

rule in dealing with them is to lead the highest and put on the lowest.* But there are marked exceptions. In all suits, with ace and king, you begin with the king; but in trumps with a major sequence of three or more, you begin with the lowest, because if the lower are not taken, your partner will infer that you have the higher; but if with three or four honors in plain suits, you begin with the queen or knave, your partner (if weak in trumps) might feel justified in trumping. Bearing in mind that the odds are four to one against a suit going round a third time without a renounce, you will see at a glance why a less venturesome course must be pursued with plain suits than with trumps; at all events, till trumps are exhausted. Thus, you play off your ace and king in a plain suit instead of beginning with a small one; with king, queen, and others, you lead the king in plain suits, and a small one in trumps.

There are some other fixed original leads (specified in the books) which must be kept in

---

* This rule does not apply to *sub*-sequences. Thus with king, ten, nine, eight, you lead the eight.

mind, not only for your own direction in leading, but to enable you to draw inferences from what your partner or adversary has led. Thus with ace and four small cards (in plain suits), the ace: with ace and three, the lowest.* With ace, queen, knave, with or without others, the ace, then the queen. With an honor and three or more small cards, or with four or more small cards (not headed by a sequence), the lowest. For leads further on in the game, you may derive important information from the discard. A good player always discards from his weak suit, or from the suit he does not wish led to him. There is no commoner or stronger sign of ignorance or inattention than instantly leading, without a defined motive, the suit from which your partner has first thrown away. As the game proceeds, also, you will of course prefer leading through the strong hand and up to the weak. Do not lead to force your partner, or on the chance of forcing him, unless you are strong in

* This is one of the points in which the best Paris players differ from the English. With ace and three small cards, they play the ace. Another is in leading from king, knave, ten *in trumps;* they lead the knave; we the ten.

trumps. We say "or on the chance of forcing," for nothing is more common than after playing ace and king, to lead a third round in the hope that the partner will win with the queen *or* trump. If he is strong in trumps, this is bad either way; for assuming him to have the best card, the odds are that it will be trumped, whereas he might have got out trumps and made it.

Mr. Clay lays down that four trumps with an honor is the minimum strength that justifies a force without a peculiar object, such as securing a double ruff or making sure of a trick to win or save the game, or unless your partner has been forced and has not led a trump, or unless he has invited the force, or unless the adversary has led or asked for trumps. "This last exception," he says, "is the slightest of the justifications for forcing your partner when you are weak in trumps, but it is in most cases a sufficient apology." We cannot think so. If the adversary has led or asked for trumps, and you are weak in them, you should do all you can to strengthen instead of weakening your partner;

instead of forcing *him*, force the trump-asking or trump-leading adversary. This is the best use of good cards when the strength in trumps has been declared against you : but take care that it is the *strong* adversary you force. "It follows that there can be but few whist offences more heinous than forcing your partner when he has led a trump (or refused to trump), and you are yourself not very strong in them."

The following is a golden rule which should prevent an infinity of hesitation : "With four trumps, do not trump an uncertain card, *i.e.*, one which your partner may be able to win. With less than four trumps, and no honor, trump an uncertain card." With a king and one, or the queen and two small trumps also, it is clearly wrong to trump an uncertain card, as it is when trumps have been played, and you have the best trump left, with a losing card to throw away. There are occasions also when it is advisable to give a trick with the view of getting led up to, but Mr. Clay says : "Do not give away a certain trick by refusing to ruff, or otherwise, unless you see a fair chance of making *two* by your forbearance." Young players should be especially cautioned against giving away sure tricks. They sometimes suffer two or three tricks to be made in a long suit by withholding the long trump, though they have nothing else to do with it.

On the other hand, eagerness to trump with strength in trumps shows ignorance or defiance of all sound principle; for you weaken yourself, and you deceive your partner, besides depriving him of the advantage of his position as fourth player, with possibly a commanding tenace. If a good player trumps a doubtful card, the inference is that he is weak in trumps; if he refuses, that he has four at least, or a guarded honor; if he refuses to trump a known winning card, take it for granted that he is strong, and at the very first opportunity lead a trump. It is usual when the ace of trumps is a singleton, to lead it at once; your partner understands that you have no more, and has the option of resuming the lead and drawing two for one. This lead cannot, like a lead from another singleton, mislead or entrap your partner.

By leading a singleton ace in a plain suit, besides inviting a force, you give up the chance of catching an adversary's honor, and the only contingency against you (an improbable one) is your partner leading the king. The lead of a singleton king is wrong, except in trumps when your partner has turned up an ace. Always consider before leading what inference your partner will be entitled to draw from your lead, and what effect it may have upon his hand, as by sacrificing one of his best cards without benefiting you.

The play of the Second Hand is more easily reducible to rule than that of the first. The cases of most frequent application are detailed in the books. Mr. Clay says :

"Playing high cards, when second to play, unless your suit is headed by two or more high cards of equal value, or unless to cover a high card, is to be carefully avoided.

"With two or three cards of the suit played, cover a high card. Play a king, or a queen, on a knave, or ten, etc.

"With four cards, or more, of the suit played, do not cover, unless the second best of your suit is also a valuable card. Thus with a king or queen, and three or more small cards, do not cover a high card ; but if, along with your king or queen, you hold the ten, or even the nine, cover a queen or a knave.

"With king and another, not being trumps, do not play your king, unless to cover a high card.

"With king and another, being trumps, play your king."

The reason he gives for this distinction is, that the ace is not generally led from except in trumps, but this is only true of the higher order of players, who see the value of an ace as a card of re-entry.

"With queen and another," he continues, "whether trumps or not, play your small card, unless to cover." Despite of this recognized maxim, many respectable players are constantly trying to snatch a trick with the queen, and exult in their occasional success; forgetting that the maxim is based on a careful calculation of the chances, and that the conventional language is confused by contravening it.

With knave, ten, or nine, and one small card, play the small card, unless to cover. With king, queen, and one or more small cards, play the queen, except in trumps, when circumstances may justify you in giving your partner a chance of making the trick. The *rationale* of the general rule, to play your lowest card second, is given by Cavendish :

"You presume that the first hand has led from strength, and if you have a high card in his suit, you lie over him when it is led again; whereas, if you play your high card second hand, you get rid of a commanding card of the adversary's suit, and when it is returned, the original leader finesses against you. Besides this the third player will put on his highest card, and, if it is better than yours, you have wasted power to no purpose."

In the first lead, therefore, if you have ace and queen with strength in trumps, you play a small card second hand, and wait for the return, the chances being that the lead is from the king. If the lead is a knave or any other card indicating weakness, put on the ace. Putting the queen (when you have ace, queen) on the knave (a common practice) is simply sacrificing her if the king is with the third player, and uselessly destroying your tenace if the king is with the fourth (your partner). The king (except in one rare contingency) must be behind you. The lead of ten or nine may be either from weakness or strength ; and (with ace, queen) you must be guided by circumstances, by the usual play of your adversary, by the state of your own hand, or (if the lead is not the first) by such indications as may have occurred.

With ace, queen, ten, play the queen. With ace, queen, knave, or with ace, queen, knave, ten, etc., the lowest of the sequence. With ace, king, knave, the king: then (in trumps, or if strong in trumps) wait for the chance of finessing or of catching the queen. With ace, king, and others in plain suits, the king; in trumps the lowest, unless you wish to stop the lead and give your partner a ruff. It is peremptorily laid down: "Play an ace on a knave." But surely this cannot be always right in trumps, for it gives up the command at once, and fulfils the precise purpose of the leader, which is presumably to clear the way for his partner. With ace and four small ones, some put on the ace second hand for the same reason which induces them to lead it with the same number of the suit. But the cases are essentially distinct; for by playing the ace second hand, you knowingly give up the advantage of lying over the leader in his strong suit. In our opinion, it should not be so played, unless you have more than four others of the suit, and are weak in trumps. By "weak" or "strong" in trumps in all such contingencies is meant, are you, or (presumably) your partner, strong enough to draw the adversary's trumps and prevent the reserved cards from being trumped? You have little chance of attaining this desirable object with less than four, including the ace or two honors, and you will probably come to grief if you attempt it with inadequate means.

The play of the Third Hand involves the theory of the finesse, on which M. Deschapelles has left a fragment which makes us regret the want of his great work as we regret the lost books of Livy or the unreported speeches of Bolingbroke. "In the high cards," he says, "the simple finesse is almost mechanical: nobody fails to practise it. There are, however, many cases which do not allow of it. We should habituate ourselves to keep the organ of attention constantly on the *qui vive*, so as only to do by choice and after balancing the advantages, the things which seem to belong to routine. A moment of distraction or forgetfulness, and you haply fall into a fault which will ruin your reputation. I have seen skilful players finesse in a trick which would have given them the game, and others commit the same blunder in the last trick but one, with a trump in. Censure has no mercy for them; its thousand sharp and quick tongues are multiplied to defame you; you cannot appear anywhere for a week without running the gauntlet of an exaggerated recital and a mortifying inquiry."

Nor is the punishment one whit too severe. In whist clubs or circles, a list of the grossest offenders should be hung up for a week, like the list of offenders against public decency in the parks, or of the defaulters or lame ducks on the Stock Exchange. We do not mean such offences as forgetting or mistaking a card, but such as forcing a partner who has led trumps or refused to trump, or finessing in the trick by which the game might be saved or won, such, in short, as the commonest discretion and the merest modicum of good sense would obviate. Habitual carelessness also merits severe reprehension, such as playing a higher card instead of a lower, even a five instead of a four, or *vice versâ*, contrary to the fixed rules of the game. The last player, not being able to win the seven, plays the six; his partner takes for granted that he has no more, refrains from a meditated lead of trumps, plays for a ruff and finds him with the five! In a trump lead, the third player with ace, six, four, three, wins with the ace, returns the four, and afterwards plays the three. His partner, taking it for granted that he has played the best of *two* remaining cards and that the remaining trump, the six, is in an adversary's hand, draws it and haply loses the game. If he had returned the three, and afterwards played the four, his partner would have known to a certainty that the remaining trump was in his hand.

To the same category belongs the playing false cards. "I hold in abhorrence the playing false cards," is the emphatic denunciation of Mr. Clay. With exceptions, which he admits, we completely go along with him; and the practice may fairly be called un-English;

for (he states), "French players are dangerously addicted to false cards, and the Americans rarely play the right card if they have one to play which is likely to deceive everybody. They play for their own hands alone—the worst fault I know in a whist-player." He puts the case of your partner winning with the highest instead of the lowest, as with the ace instead of the king, whence you assume that the king is against you and find the whole scheme of your game destroyed. But take the every-day case—with the king led presumably from ace and king—of dropping the queen instead of the knave, in the hope of stopping the suit. The suit is stopped, but your partner may be mischievously deceived; for, on your having or not having the knave, depends the entire quality of your hand and the course of combined action he should pursue. False cards, therefore should never be played unless at a period of the game when your partner is practically *hors de combat*, or when he is incapable of drawing the ordinary inferences which will be drawn by your adversaries. "Why did you play that card?" was the question incautiously put to a good player by an astonished bystander. "For the very sufficient reason," was the answer, in a loud stage whisper, "that my partner is a *muff.*"

Habitual hesitation, also, is a very grave fault. It is by turns unfair as enlightening your partner and indiscreet as giving hints to your adversaries. Indicating the quality of the hand in any manner, by word or gesture, should be suppressed by a penalty; and any player who says he has the game in his hand, should lay his cards on the table and submit to have them called. Cards thrown down should always be called, for otherwise an unfair advantage is obtained; all liability to a mistake in playing them being thereby avoided; and the practice should be discountenanced as wasting instead of saving both time and temper by the discussion it creates. Like Mrs. Battle we are decidedly for "a clear fire, a clean hearth, and the rigor of the game." * Unless the laws are

* *Elia.* First Series —Hazlitt, although, like a certain dignified ornament of the church, constantly in hot water, was not equally remarkable for clean hands.

regularly enforced, any occasional enforcement of them is open to the imputation of an unfair advantage; so that uniform strictness is most favorable to a good understanding.

A moment's pause before the opening—and no good player will need more—for the formation of a plan is not to be confounded with hesitation. "This moment," observes M. Deschapelles, "will be amply compensated: it may save ten; for the cards will flow rapidly as consequences; your adversaries will be unable to draw inferences; and your partner, catching confidence from your self-possession, will become charged with the electric spark which fuses the *moi* into the intelligent and co-operating *nous*."

But we are digressing and must return to the finesse, which depends so much on inference and the state of the score, that few general maxims can be laid down. *Imprimis*, the only finesse permissible in your partner's long suit (his first lead) is from ace and queen. If the

Elia (Charles Lamb), playing whist with him, dryly observed: "If dirt was trumps, what hands you would hold."

queen wins, immediately return the ace in trumps, and also in plain suits, unless there are symptoms of trumping. In that case, play trumps, if you are strong enough; otherwise change the suit, and wait to see what your partner will do; or, if you have a good trump, though weak, play it to strengthen him. A good player will, of course, finesse more frequently, and more deeply, in trumps than in plain suits, because he is generally sure of making the reserved card, and of making it at the most favorable moment. Thus, if with ace, king, and knave, he finesses the knave and loses it, he is still in a better position than if he had played his king and left the queen guarded and held up behind him. With ace, knave, ten (in trumps), the ten may be finessed if two immediate rounds are not required. When weak in trumps, finesse deeply in the suit in which your partner is weak. This, though contrary to the general practice, is strongly recommended by Mr. Clay. The finesse of knave from king, knave, cannot be recommended unless your partner has obviously led from weakness. Your partner wins with the queen and returns the lead with a small card: with king, ten, finesse the ten, for the ace is certainly held over you, and if the knave is in the same hand, you must lose both any way. This is an instance of what is called the finesse obligatory.

The chief difficulty of the Fourth Hand is in discriminating the rare instances in which the trick should not be taken. You have three cards left: ace, knave, and a small one; your adversary with king, queen, ten, leads the king. If you take the king, you win one trick; if you allow it to make, you win two. There are also occasions when you give the trick in order to compel the adversary to lead up to you in another suit. A common *ruse* (which Mr. Clay strongly condemns) is to hold up the ace when you have ace and knave and the adversary has led the king from king and queen. This is dangerous out of trumps, or unless you are very strong in trumps and want to establish the suit, and then your partner may trump the second round and be carried off on a wrong scent. In trumps, the opportunity can rarely arise with good players. An ace may sometimes be kept back with telling effect, not only in trumps, but with ace and four small cards in a plain suit; the trumps being out or with you, and three tricks required to win or save the game. If no other player has more than three, and the ace is kept back till the third round, the three tricks are secured.

But an inexperienced player cannot be recommended to risk a stroke of this kind; neither should we recommend him to resort to *underplay*, until he has advanced far enough to be initiated into the mysteries of the *grand coup*.* Play the plain, unpretending, unambitious game, till the higher and finer class of combinations break upon you. On the other hand, don't shun any amount of justifiable risk. If, looking to the score and the number of tricks

---

* The *grand coup* is getting rid of a superfluous trump which may compel you to win a trick and take the lead when you do not want it. It was the master-stroke, the *coup de Jarnac*, of Deschapelles. *Underplay* is when, retaining the best of a suit, you play a small one in the hope that your left-hand adversary will hold up the second best and allow your partner to make the trick with a lower card.

on the table, a desperate measure is called for, risk it; if great strength in trumps in your partner's hand is required to save the game, play your best trump, however weak in them. All ordinary rules must be set aside in this emergency; every available force must be instantly called into the field. Here is the crisis in which you must lead the king with only one small one in his train: as at Fontenoy and Steinkirk, there is nothing for it but for the *maison du roi* to charge. There are moments in whist when a *coup d'œil* is wanted like that of the dying Marmion:

> " Let Stanley charge with spur of fire,
> With Chester charge and Lancashire,
> Full upon Scotland's central host,
> Or victory and England's lost."

One of the chosen few being asked what he deemed the distinctive excellence of a fine player, replied, "playing to the point." Such a player plays almost every hand differently without once departing from the conventional language of the game. It is an excellence rarely attained or appreciated; and the great majority of players play on just the same whatever the state of the score or the number of tricks already made on either side. They not only run risks to secure three tricks when they only want one : we have seen a gentleman playing for the odd trick with six tricks made against him, deliberately give away the seventh by declining to trump for fear of being overtrumped! We have seen another take out the card that would have won the game, look at it, fumble with it, and then put it back again. Nelson told his captains at Trafalgar that any one of them who did not see his way clearly could not go far wrong if he laid his ship alongside a ship of the enemy. No whist-player can go far wrong who wins a trick when the game is growing critical. We do not say with Hoyle: "Whenever you are in doubt, win the trick"; for we have heard puzzle-headed people appeal to this maxim after trumping the leading card of their partner's long suit, or trumping a doubtful card with the solitary guard to a king or with one of four trumps which constituted their strength. But we say : when you are in doubt with the adverse pack of tricks dangerously mounting up, win the trick. Hesitation without knowledge makes matters worse. Instead of snatching a grace beyond the reach of art, the hesitating player commonly commits a blunder beyond the reach of speculation, and tempts one to exclaim with Johnson: "You must have taken great pains with yourself, sir; you could not naturally have been so very stupid."

Few readers can have forgotten the bitter comment of Rasselas after Imlac had enumerated the qualities needed to excel in poetry: "Enough, thou hast convinced me that no human being can ever be a poet." An enumeration of the qualities needed to shine in whist might provoke a similar retort. In the famous passage which Mr. Disraeli borrowed from M. Thiers, describing the qualifications and responsibilities of a great commander, we find: "At the same moment he must think of the eve and the morrow—of his flanks and his reserve: he must calculate at the same time the state of the weather and the moral qualities of his men. * * * Not only must he think —he must think with the rapidity of lightning; for on a moment more or less depends the fate of the finest combinations, and on a moment more or less depends the glory or the shame. Doubtless all this may be done in an ordinary manner by an ordinary man ; as we see every day of our lives ordinary men making successful ministers of state, successful speakers, successful authors. But to do all this with genius is sublime."

Something very similar might be said of a great whist-player,—indeed, has been said by M. Deschapelles, who was himself the great sublime he drew. He must watch and draw inferences from three hands besides his own ; he must play twenty-six cards instead of thirteen ; he must follow the shifting condition of four suits ; he must calculate, at the same time, each phase of the game, and the moral and mental qualities of the players. Are they strong or weak, bold or cautious, frank or tricky and given to false cards ? He must think with intuitive rapidity and sagacity. If he miscalculates, or loses the key to a single combination, he is lost. We see ordinary men making tolerably good whist-players, but the fine whist-player is as rare as the great commander; and to the *beau idéal* one might be applied what the Irishman predicated of a finished Irish gentleman—that there would be nothing like him in the world, *if you could but meet with him.*

Not only did we never meet with or hear of a whist-player who could venture to boast with Turenne that he never fought a battle that he did not deserve to win; but we have heard an excellent one adopt the aphorism, attributed to the Iron Duke, that a battle was a game in which those who made the fewest blunders won. Or a parallel may be drawn between the paladin of the whist-table and the damsel in the Vaudeville who took her married sister's fault upon herself, and is thus apostrophized by her brother-in-law : "Quoi! vous, Marie, vous, la Vertu même!" Her reply is exquisite for feminine self-knowledge and tact : "Oh! la Vertu, la Vertu! tout le monde a ses heures ou ses moments." The most consummate skill, like Virtue herself, is not safe against a slip. Did not the late Earl Granville lose a rubber, after giving the long odds in thousands, by forgetting the seven of hearts? Did not Henry Lord de Roos lose one on which three thousand pounds was staked by miscounting a trump? Did not, only the other day, the Daniel or Gamaliel of the Arlington fail to detect a palpable revoke, to the astonishment and (it must be owned) gratification of the by-standers, some of whom went home consoled and elevated in their own self-esteem by his default?

But let no one hurry to the conclusion that skill is of minor importance because it is sometimes found tripping, or because the fine player may be often seen vainly struggling against cards, when, like the good man struggling against adversity, he is a spectacle for the gods. "Human life," writes Jeremy Taylor, "is like playing at tables; the luck is not in our power, but the playing the game is." For "playing at tables," read whist. Independently of the intellectual gratification, skill will prove an ample and material remuneration in the long run for the pains bestowed in acquiring it. If only one trick per hand were won or lost by play, the percentage would be immense; but two or three tricks per hand are frequently so won or lost. We have repeatedly in a single sitting seen bad players score three or four with hands which, held by good players, would infallibly have made the game. With tolerably equal cards, play must turn the balance : with fortune *pro*, it indefinitely increases the gain ; with fortune *con*, it indefinitely diminishes the loss. It must have been the effect of irritability after losing to bunglers that made high authorities deny so obvious a truth. We are quite sure that in their cooler moments they would agree with us.

A curious piece of evidence bearing on this subject was given at the De Roos trial by a distinguished whist-player, who stated that he had played regularly for about the same stakes during twenty years; that his winnings had averaged £1,500 a year, making £30,000 in the aggregate, but that he had two consecutive years of ill-luck, during which he lost £8,000. Another witness, a captain in the navy, who had realized a regular income by his skill, was asked whether he was not in the habit of dining on boiled chicken and lemonade when he had serious work in hand; and the alleged training (which he denied) was no imputation on his sagacity. No man flushed with food or wine, *vinoque ciboque gravatus*, will play his best.

Although many of the best players play high, the highest players are by no means uniformly the best. It was stated from melancholy experience by De Quincey, that opium-eating in the earlier stages produces none of the beneficial or pleasurable effects; not till it has grown into a habit does the inspiring or soothing influence begin. It is the same with high play, which unduly excites and agitates for a season; although, if the purse and constitution hold out, it has been known to sharpen the observation and concentrate the attention to the utmost point which the player's natural capabilities enable him to reach. But this turning a relaxation and a pleasure into a business and a toil, is to be deprecated, not recommended; and a wise man (pecuniary considerations apart) would rather give up whist altogether, than be compelled to play it under the implied condition that he was to keep his mind eternally upon the strain. It was this consideration possibly that drove Charles James Fox to hazard, although he boasted that he could gain £4,000 a year at whist if he chose to set about it. Major Aubrey, who had tried both, declared that the greatest pleasure in life was winning at whist,—the next greatest pleasure, losing.

Women, particularly young women, should never play for sums which it is inconvenient to them to lose; and a sum which is immaterial to a man of independent means may create an alarming deficit in a female budget dependent on an allowance of pin-money. The feminine organization is opposed to their ever getting beyond the excitable perturbed fluttered stage: their hands may be read in their faces; they play recklessly to shorten the torment of suspense; and it is fortunate if, along with their money, they do not lose both their temper and their good looks:

> " And one degrading hour of sordid fear,
> Stamp in a night the wrinkles of a year."

The charge of comparative disregard of truth which the male sex, with or without reason, are wont to bring against the female, derives plausibility from an effect stated by Byron:

> " The pretty creatures fib with such a grace,
> There's nothing so becoming to the face."

Upon this principle they should certainly avoid high play at any game, for there is nothing so *un*becoming to the face. Hogarth's print of *The Lady's Lost Stake* suggests another danger, which is also hinted at in *The Provoked Husband:*

"*Lord Townley:* 'Tis not your ill hours that always disturb me, but as often the ill company that occasion these hours.

"*Lady Townley:* Sure, I don't understand you now, my lord. What ill company do I keep?

"*Lord Townley:* Why, at best, women that lose their money, and men that win it; or perhaps men that are voluntary bubbles at one game in hopes a lady will give them fair play at another."

When whist is merely taken up as one of the weapons of coquetry, there is no great mischief to be apprehended; although *écarté* or chess would seem more suited to the purpose, and give better hope of a situation like that of Ferdinand and Miranda. "Sweet lord, you play me false," is ill replaced by "Sweet lady, you have revoked."

Henri Beyle (Stendhal), musing over an interrupted *liaison* and a lost illusion, exclaims: "After all, her conduct is rational. She was fond of whist. She is fond of it no longer: so much the worse for me if I am still fond of whist." So much the better for him, as he had still an inexhaustible resource; and he would have gained nothing by abandoning it. She was no longer fond of whist, because she was no longer fond of him.

It is a common fallacy, mischievously rife amongst the fair sex, that without the gift of extraordinary memory, it is impossible to become a good whist-player; the fact being that memory has little or nothing to do with the real understanding or finest points of the game. What, for instance, has memory to do with the opening lead, which has the same relative importance that Lord Lyndhurst attributed to the opening speech in a cause? What has memory to do with trumping or not trumping a doubtful card; or with returning the best with three and the lowest with four; or with returning the trump lead immediately; or with answering the call for trumps; or with taking the trick that wins or saves the game; or with numberless emergencies in which you have only to look at your hand, the tricks on the table, and the score?

Of course a certain number of rules and maxims must be learnt; but it is not more difficult to learn these than to learn the Catechism; and a lady might as reasonably complain that she could not become a good Christian for want of memory, as that she could not become a good whist-player by reason of that defect; which, in nine cases out of ten, is purely imaginary. People remember well enough what they care to remember, or what fixes their attention by interesting them. This depends on character, habits, and powers of appreciation. Whilst the man of cultivated taste and fine sense of humor is laying up a stock of choice anecdotes and fine passages, an old maid in a country town will be growing into the living chronicle of all the scandalous gossip of the last fifty years, complaining all the time of her memory. The measures are the same, but the one is filled with pearls of price, and the other with glass beads and knicknackery. The discriminating reminiscent, instead of being envied for memory, should be commended for refined observation, judgment, quickness of perception, and *apropos*.

Alleged forgetfulness at whist, as in most other things, is far more frequently inattention than forgetfulness. The fall of the cards has not been watched, and the proper inferences have not been drawn at the moment. A player cannot be said to have forgotten what he never knew. If, for example, at the end of a second round, he had clearly drawn the inference that the best card remained with one adversary and that the other had no more of the suit, this state of things would suggest itself naturally and without any effort when the suit was played again :

"With care [says Mr. Clay] and with his eyes never wandering from the table, each day will add to the indications which he will observe and understand. He will find that mere memory has less to do with whist than he imagines, that it matters little whether the five or the six is the best card left of a suit, as long as he knows, which he generally ought to know, who has that best card. Memory and observation will become mechanical to him, and cost him little effort, and all that remains for him to do will be to calculate at his ease the best way of playing his own and his partner's hands, in many cases as if he saw the greater portion of the cards laid face upwards on the table. He will then be a fine whist-player."

Without being a fine whist-player, he may be a capital second-rate, a thoroughly reliable partner, and one with whom no one can be dissatisfied to sit down. This is the grand point, and this (we repeat) may be attained with no more than the average amount of memory with which men and women manage to get on creditably through life. One of the confessedly best London whist-players is below the average in this particular. Nor will calling him so appear paradoxical to any who accept M. Deschapelles' division :

"We will suppose a parabola described by a bombshell, of which the culminating point shall be the seventh trick. On this side, it is invention which holds sway; on the other, it is calculation. Attention and memory are at the base, whilst sagacity, seated at the top, distributes the work, calls by turns on the organs that are to complete it, excites and circumscribes their efforts, and assigns them at the appointed moment the repose necessary to the restoration of their strength. * * * When there are no more than five or six cards remaining in the hand, the fine and delicate faculties of intelligence have resigned and repose. Mathematical calculation is at the helm: the simplest calculation disengaged from the unknown. Then it is that the most commonplace player is entitled to claim equality with the finest; it is a property which he has acquired by his labor; the elements of it are open to all the world. They are beyond the domain of the aristocracy of the brain and the susceptibility of the organs; beyond that of poetry and imagination; but they are open to all, like the right to breathe and speak good prose! * * * With regard to sagacity, how do you know that you are wanting in it? Do but apply your mind to the matter in hand, *age quod agis*, and you will see that you have as much as another. I can give as proof the manner in which people lead at present; even at our weakest parties, I am surprised to see that it is almost always the right card that is led. This is owing to our *grande tactique*, with which every one is imbued."

The *grande tactique* is the strong or long-suit system; with which, we regret to say, every one is not imbued amongst us, or we should not so frequently hear, at the end of a long, puzzled, and unreflecting pause, "I really do not know what to lead." The lady or gentleman who habitually indulges in this apostrophe, had better say at once, "I really do not know how to play."

Every civilized country has had its Augustan age or ages. We have had our Elizabethan age, our age of Queen Anne, and what was also an Augustan age, though yet unnamed—the age when Byron, Moore, Scott, Wordsworth, Coleridge, Rogers, Sydney Smith, Hallam, Brougham, Canning, etc., were the central figures of the group. On its being recently remarked that there was nothing now coming on to replace what must be soon passing away— that almost all the highest reputations in all walks are of full twenty years' standing or more; that we have no rising poets, artists, novelists, or orators,—"No!" exclaimed a far-famed beauty and wit, "and no lady-killers such as I remember in my heyday, before whom one felt bound to succumb, as the belles of the *Spectator* succumbed to Beau Fielding, when he said of them: 'Elles tombent comme des mouches.'" Our fair friend, who is also a competent judge on this subject, might have added: "And no rising whist-players of the first class; not one under middle age, who has given proofs of undisputed genius."

A master of the art who has survived a generation, was recently asked who were the best whist-players he ever knew. He instantly named three: the late Earl Granville, the Hon. George Anson, and Henry Lord de Roos. On being asked for the fourth he paused, but there was no need of hesitation: "Ed io anche sono pittore." No one would have accused him of undue assumption if he had followed the example of Lamartine, who, on being asked who was the first living French poet, drew himself up with an air of offended dignity, and replied, "Moi." The palm is popularly considered to lie between Lord Henry Bentinck and Mr. Clay; whose styles are so essentially different that an instructive parallel might be drawn between them after the manner of Plutarch.

The de Roos affair was a sad blow and a temporary discredit to whist-players, for some of them were unluckily seduced into acting on the late Lord Hertford's maxim: "What would you do if you saw a man cheating at cards?" "Bet upon him, to be sure." Lord de Roos' methods of aiding his skill were only available for one hand in four—when he dealt. He then contrived to turn an honor by what is called *sauter le coup*, and having marked the higher honors with his nail, he could see to whom they fell. During the burst of scandalous comment which followed the exposure, one of the "bitter fools" of society, who had never been admitted to his intimacy, drawled out at Crockford's: "I would leave my card at his house, but I fear he would mark it." The retort was ready: "That would depend on whether he considered it a *high* honor." This repartee, popularly assigned to Lord Alvanley—*on ne prête qu'aux riches*—was made by Charles Kinnaird Sheridan (the brother of the three gifted sisters of the race), whose untimely and deeply regretted death, in the bloom of his brilliant youth, was a *memento mori* which not the gayest or most thoughtless of his gay contemporaries could speedily shake off.

"Manibus date lilia plenis:
Purpureos spargam flores, animamque nepotis
His saltem accumulem donis, et fungar inani
Munere."

There is a well authenticated story of Lord Granville's devotion to whist. Intending to set out in the course of the afternoon for Paris, he ordered his carriage and four posters to be at Graham's at four. They were kept waiting till ten, when he sent out to say that he should not be ready for another hour or two and that the horses had better be changed; they were changed three times in all, at intervals of six hours, before he started. When the party rose, they were up to their ankles in cards, and the ambassador (it was reported) was a loser to the tune of eight or ten thousand pounds. About this time there was a set at Brookes' (Lord Sefton, an excellent player, being one) who played hundred-guinea points besides bets. We still occasionally hear of £300 and £500 on the rubber, but five-pound points are above the average; and many of the best players are content with two-pound points (ten, bet) at the Arlington, and half pounds at the Portland. A great deal of money is turned on the five to two (really nearer three to one) bet on the rubber after the first game.

In Paris (where the rubber counts four) the points are comparatively low, much in our opinion to the detriment of the game. During the period comprised in M. Louis Blanc's *Histoire des Dix Ans*, the stakes at the Cercle de l'Union were such that Count Achille Delamarre calculated his average rubber at 200 louis. There, and afterwards at the Jockey Club, the level rate was two louis and ten bet, but the large *ad libitum* bets became so general that any one who cut in without joining in them was looked upon as an interloper. The principal players at the Union were Lord Granville (the English ambassador), Count Meden (the Russian ambassador), Comte Walewski, the Duc de Richelieu, General Michelski, Comte Deschapelles (the author), Comte Achille Delamarre, and M. Bonpierre; the three last, with Lord Granville, being esteemed the best of the lot. Amongst the best Parisian players who have subsequently come into the field (of green cloth), are Vicomte Paul Daru, Comte d'Albon, Comte d'Andlau, Comte de Malart, Vicomte Ladislas de St.-Pierre, and his brother M. Maurice de St.-Pierre. The highest play during the last two or three years has been at the Petit Club de la Rue Royale, where it ranges from 1 and 30, or 1 and 50, up to or about 1 and 100 louis; the points being stationary and the bets fluctuating. The scale of play has been recently raised above the usual level at Paris by the very high play at baccarat, at which £16,000 has been lost by one person in one night.

There used to be high play at Berlin· and Vienna. Count Palfy won enough at a single sitting of Prince John of Lichtenstein to build and furnish a *château*. It was shown to the loser, who on being asked how he liked it, replied: "Pas du tout; cela a tout à fait l'air d'un château de cartes." Count Brühl wrote a treatise on whist, which, we regret to say, we have been unable to procure in time for this article. There is a current anecdote of Count Rechberg, late Secretary for Foreign Affairs in Austria, which justifies a surmise that he also is a proficient.

His left-hand adversary (*proh pudor* an Englishman) made so desperate though successful a finesse, that his Excellency uttered an exclamation of surprise; whereupon the gentleman offered a bet that the Count himself should acknowledge that he had a sound reason for his play. It was taken, and he then coolly said: "Why, I looked over your hand." This gentleman must have graduated under the Artful Dodger, who, when playing dummy in Fagan's den, is commended for "wisely regulating his play by the result of his observations on his neighbors' cards."

Some thirty years since a remarkable set used to meet in Berlin at Prince Wittgenstein's, including Count Alopeus, the Russian Minister, General Nostitz, Sir Henry Bulwer (then attached to the Berlin embassy), and the Duke of Cumberland (afterwards King of Hanover). Another of the royal family, the late Duke of York, played whist a great deal and lost a great deal of money at it, as well he might, for he invariably showed whether he was satisfied or dissatisfied with his cards, and played them indifferently into the bargain. He played pony points (£25) and fifty bet, making the full or bumper rubber £250. One evening, having won three full rubbers of a wealthy *parvenu*. he was reluctantly reminded that there was a prior loss of some four thousand pounds to be set off. "No, no," he protested, "that will never do. We have nothing to do with old scores"; and the man was fool enough to pay. There is no royal road to whist, and as royal personages with the best natural dispositions rarely submit to be taught, it is fortunate that the kingly power has been limited since Canute, who had a courtier hanged for checkmating him, and would doubtless have had him hanged, drawn, and quartered for claiming a revoke at whist. This great and wise king had evidently come to the conclusion that the occasional execution of a courtier *pour encourager les autres* inculcated a moral more practically than getting wet feet through the disobedience of the waves.

When Napoleon was at Würtemberg, "he used to play whist in the evening, but not for money, playing ill and inattentively. One evening when the queen dowager was playing with him against her husband and his daughter (the Queen of Westphalia, the wife of Jerome), the King stopped Napoleon, who was taking up a trick that belonged to them, saying: 'Sire, on ne joue pas ici en conquérant.' " *

It must be admitted as a partial excuse for absolutism in such matters, that the spirit of play absorbs or deadens every other thought and feeling. Horace Walpole relates that, on a man falling down in a fit before the bay window of White's, odds were instantly offered and taken to a large amount against his recovery, and that, on its being proposed to bleed him, the operation was vehemently resisted as

* *Diaries of the Lady of Quality*, second edition, p. 128. Frederic the Great was in the habit of kicking the shins of the *savans* who ventured to differ from him. When Peter the Great was on a visit of inspection on board an English line-of-battle ship at Portsmouth, he expressed a wish to witness the operation of *keel-hauling;* which consists in dragging the subject under water from one side of the ship to the other by means of a rope passed under the keel. He was told that this was contrary to law, so far as Englishmen were concerned. "If that is all, you can take one of my suite," was his unconcerned rejoinder. It would be pleasing to watch the countenance of Sir Edward Cust, or General Grey, or one of the Lords in Waiting, when told off for such an experiment by our gracious Sovereign.

unfair. When Lord Thanet was in the Tower for the O'Connor riot, three friends were admitted to play whist with him, and remain till the lock-up hour of eleven. Early in the sitting his partner fell back in a fit of apoplexy, and one of the party rose to call for help. "Stop," cried another, "we shall be turned out if you make a noise; let our friend alone till eleven; we can play dummy, and he'll be none the worse, for I can read death in his face."

The profession of medicine has turned out some good whist-players. Three celebrated physicians, being, like the surgeons in *Zeluco*, at a loss how to fill up the time it was thought decent to occupy on the case of a noble patient, set to at dummy. The patient, if there had really been much the matter with him, would have found himself in the predicament of the survivor of the Horatii :

" Que vouliez-vous qu'il fît contre trois ?
Qu'il mourût."

The clergy, especially in the West of England, were formerly devoted to whist. About the beginning of the century there was a whist club in a country town of Somersetshire, composed mostly of clergymen, that met every Sunday evening in the back parlor of a barber. Four of these were acting as pall-bearers at the funeral of a reverent brother, when a delay occurred, from the grave not being ready, or some other cause, and the coffin was set down in the chancel. By way of whiling away the time, one of them produced a pack of cards from his pocket and proposed a rubber. The rest gladly assented, and they were deep in their game, using the coffin as their table, when the sexton came to announce that the preparations were complete. We have carefully verified the fact that they played long whist, and we suspect that whist has been less popular in the church since the introduction of short, by reason of its inferior gravity. The principle is indicated by Sydney Smith in his qualified defence of angling. "I give up fly-fishing; it is a light, volatile, dissipated pursuit. But ground-bait, with a good steady float that never bobs without a bite, is an occupation for a bishop, and in no way interferes with sermon-making."

We have seen short whist played by a member of the episcopal body, and a very eminent one, the venerable Bishop of Exeter (Phillpotts), one adversary being the late Dean of St. Paul's (Milman), the other an American diplomatist, and his partner a distinguished foreigner whose whist is hardly on a par with his scientific acquirements and social popularity. The two dignitaries played a steady, sound orthodox game. The Bishop bore a run of ill luck like a Christian and a bishop, but when (after the diplomatist had puzzled him by a false card) the Count lost the game by not returning his trump, the excellent prelate looked on the verge of bringing the rubber to a conclusion as he once brought a controversy with an archbishop, namely, by the bestowal of his blessing; which the archbishop, apparently apprehensive of its acting by the rule of contraries, earnestly entreated him to take back.

The famous " Billy Butler," vicar of Frampton, got the offer of a rich piece of preferment by finding a fox in the "open" when the Prince of Wales (afterwards George IV.) was anxious for an easy run. Many a good living has been gained by whist-playing, this being considered an indispensable qualification by discerning patrons (lay and episcopal) in the olden time. Our own opinion is that, if the spirit of the times no longer admits of its being exacted in candidates for holy orders, the being well up in Cavendish or Clay should command a handsome number of marks in all competitive examinations, civil and military. We throw out this suggestion for the serious consideration of the Cabinet; especially of Mr. Gladstone, Mr. Bright, and Mr. Lowe.

ABRAHAM HAYWARD,
in *Fraser's Magazine.*

THE THIRTY-NINE ARTICLES OF WHIST.*

THE following Rules of Whist are based on the principle of American Leads as developed by "Cavendish," and Mr. N. B. Trist, of New Orleans, and are compiled for players who have some knowledge of the game. The chief features of the American Leads are as follows: 1. A low card led indicates three cards higher than the one led. 2. A high card led, followed by a low one, indicates two cards remaining, higher than the second card led. 3. A high card led, followed by another high card, always gives some information as to the number of cards in the suit: sometimes the exact number.

ORIGINAL LEADS.

1. The best tactics at Whist aim at establishing a long suit, in order to bring in the remaining cards after

* By the courtesy of Richard Irving Dunbar.

trumps have been exhausted. Therefore the original lead should be from the longest suit, unless that suit be of four cards only, headed by one lower than the Nine.

2. The lead of the ACE indicates length (that is, at least five cards), or Queen-Knave. Always lead Ace with more than four in suit, except with head sequence.

> If you have already trumped, however, always lead Ace with Ace-King, irrespective of length. If your partner be short, he might trump in order to establish a cross-ruff.

3. The KING indicates Ace or Queen (or both), and never more than four in the suit.

4. The QUEEN indicates Ace-King and length, King and length, or the head of a sequence.

5. The KNAVE indicates sequence to King or Ace, with length; or the highest of a short suit.

6. The TEN indicates King and Knave, with or without the Nine; or the highest of a short suit.

7. In all other cases the FOURTH-BEST is led.

8. If you open a long suit after trumps have been exhausted, usually lead as in trumps (*q. v.*).

9. Should the long suit be of four cards headed by one lower than the Nine, open the best three-card suit, one in sequence if possible; generally leading the highest, except when holding a Tenace; or Ace and Knave; or Ace, King, or Queen, as the only high card: then lead the lowest.

> Always lead the highest of a short suit, if the previous play has shown it to be your partner's long suit.

SUBSEQUENT LEADS.

10. If following up original lead, usually play the *best* card.

11. If without the *best* card, follow with *original* fourth-best, unless having held originally three or more high cards: then lead one of the remaining high cards.

> But, with King-Queen and length, if the Queen win, follow with fourth-best of the *remaining* cards.

12. After leading a high card, if left with two or three high cards that are "indifferent" (that is, of equal trick-taking value), show length in suit by leading the lower; *e. g.*, (a) with Ace-Queen-Knave, lead Ace and follow with Queen if having held originally three or four; and with Knave if having held five or more; (b) with King-Queen-Knave and length, lead Knave (even if one of the other cards be the Ten); follow with King if having held five; with Queen if having held six or more.

13. The Ace as a secondary lead, followed by the King, indicates no more in the suit and a desire to ruff.

TRUMP LEADS.

14. The best use to which you can put a strong trump suit is to play it out, to remove the only obstacle to making tricks in the long plain suits.

15. With seven or more trumps, usually lead as in plain suits. With less than seven, lead the fourth-

best, unless with at least three honors. Exceptions: (a) with King-Queen-Ten and two or more small cards, lead Queen; if without the Ten, lead fourth-best, unless with seven in the suit; (b) lead the highest of a sequence, headed by Queen or Knave, regardless of length.

The turn-up card may also modify the lead. And, of course, you may *finesse* more deeply in trumps than in plain suits.

16. Make trumps your original lead, having five or more, even if without an honor, except when void in a suit or with a singleton. But, with five small trumps, a moderate plain suit, and no high cards in the other suits, it is better to lead from the long plain suit, unless your partner has shown strength.

17. Rarely lead from a suit of four trumps unless very strong in other suits, or with three cards in each, or until you have established a suit.

> Be cautious in leading trumps if your adversaries have also established a suit. Under these conditions, success will follow the side that first forces the strong hand.
> Should your first lead be after an adversary has established a long strong suit, or after your partner has opened a four-card or weak long suit, generally do not lead trumps, even if strong in them, but try to utilize your partner's trumps by forcing him.

18. Lead trumps, when weak in them, only when holding commanding strength in all plain suits, or to stop a cross-ruff. But having a very poor hand, with the score against you, 3—0 or 4—0, generally lead trumps: for unless your partner has a strong hand the game is lost.

RETURN LEADS.

19. Usually return at once your partner's lead, except (a) when you have a strong suit of your own; (b) when you have taken the trick cheaply; (c) when your trump suit is strong enough to warrant opening it.

20. Having held originally three cards in your partner's suit, return the higher; having held more, return the lowest.

> If left with the *best* card, however, always play it; or if with second- and third-best, always return the highest, irrespective of length.

PLAY OF SECOND HAND.

21. Usually play lowest card, second hand.

22. Holding cards such that you would, if first player, lead high, usually play high, second hand; except with Ace and four small cards. Play the lowest of indifferent high cards.

23. Holding Ace, Queen and more, play Queen only when Nine or Ten is led, unless very long in suit and weak in trumps.

24. Holding Ace-Queen-Ten, usually play Queen when any low card is led; except in trumps, when play Ten.

25. Cover an honor with the *best* card *only*, unless you hold a "fourchette," *i. e.*, a card next higher and one next lower than the card led, when always cover.

26. Holding King and one small card, play King only when Nine is led; or the Eight, when your small card is the Nine.

27. Holding Queen and one small card, play Queen only when Nine or Ten is led.

28. The fourth-best card of a suit being led, the leader holds three cards higher. If the number of pips on the card thus led be subtracted from *eleven*, the remainder will be the number of cards out against the leader, higher than the card led. When a fourth-best card is led, therefore, if the number of pips on that card added to the number of higher cards held by you makes eleven, cover with the lowest of the high cards, since you hold all the high cards not in the leader's hand.*

The rule is the same when Ace is led, followed by the original fourth-best.

29. Holding *best* card in the second round of a suit, usually play it.

PLAY OF THIRD HAND.

30. Generally play your best card on your partner's original lead.

31. But, with Ace and Queen, play Queen. This is an imperative *finesse*.

32. Never play Ace on partner's lead of King or Queen; but if holding only one other card, Ace may be played on Knave.

33. Rarely play Queen on your partner's lead of Nine, and never on his lead of Ten.

34. But always avoid being left after the second round

---

* This rule was first worked out by Mr. R. F. Foster, of New York, and afterwards independently discovered by Mr. E. F. M. Benecke, of Oxford, England, who was the first to make it public.

with the best card only of your partner's suit, if he has shown length as well as strength. Therefore, with three cards originally, take the second trick; with four cards, retain the lowest as long as you can.

35. Rarely *finesse* in the second round, holding best and third best.

THE SIGNAL.

36. When you wish your partner to lead trumps, throw an unnecessarily high card on his or the adversary's lead, following it with a lower card when you next play a card of the same suit.

37. In answering a call for trumps, lead the highest of two or three cards, the lowest of four or more; unless holding the Ace, which should always be led.

THE ECHO.

38. When your partner has called for trumps and you have numerical strength, you should also call if opportunity offer. If you trump with a card higher than that which you afterward play, he will understand that you held four or more trumps originally.

THE DISCARD.

39. The original discard should always be from the weakest suit, unless great strength in trumps has been declared against you; when discard from your best protected suit. This rule generally holds good even if your partner has also shown strength in trumps.

Remember that indication of suit is given by *original discard only*.

The Thirty-nine Articles of Whist

GENERAL REMARKS.

A. Endeavor to play in harmony with your partner; that is, never consider your own hand as separate from his.

B. It is better to inform your partner than to deceive your adversary; therefore rarely play a false card.

C. Your first object should be to save the game, if it appear in danger; your next to win it, if you have a reasonable chance of success.

D. Never play a singleton as original lead.

E. Rarely force your partner unless you hold four trumps, including an honor; or unless your partner has shown weakness in trumps.

F. Force the adversary's strong trump hand, unless both adversaries have renounced.

G. If strong in trumps rarely trump a doubtful card, but trump fearlessly if weak.

H. If your partner refuse to trump a sure winning card, lead trumps.

I. When you have nothing better to do, lead up to the weak, or through the strong hand of the adversary.

J. In playing for the odd trick, the violation of established rules is *sometimes* justifiable; *e. g.*, leading a singleton; forcing your partner when weak in trumps; refraining from leading trumps when very strong; refusing to *finesse;* playing a false card; etc.

RICHARD IRVING DUNBAR.

RHYMING RULES, MNEMONIC MAXIMS, AND POCKET PRECEPTS.

BEING SHORT MEMORANDA OF IMPORTANT POINTS TO BE KEPT IN MIND BY THOSE WHO WOULD PRACTISE THE MODERN SCIENTIFIC GAME OF WHIST.

IF you the modern game of whist would know,
From this great principle its precepts flow :
Treat your own hand as to your partner's joined,
And play, not one alone, but *both combined*.

Your first lead makes your partner understand
What is the chief component of your hand ;
And hence there is necessity the strongest,
That *your first lead be from your suit that's longest*.

In this, with *ace* and *king*, lead *king*, then *ace*;
With *king* and *queen*, *king* also has first place;
With *ace, queen, knave*, lead *ace* and then the *queen;*
With *ace, four small ones, ace* should first be seen;
With *queen, knave, ten*, you let the *queen* precede;
In other cases you the lowest lead.

Ere you return your friend's, your *own* suit play;
But *trumps you must return without delay.*

When you return your partner's lead, take pains
To lead him back the *best* your hand contains,
If you received *not more than three* at first;
If you had more, you may return the worst.

But if you hold the *master card* you 're bound
In most cases to play it *second round.*

Whene'er you want a lead, 'tis seldom wrong
To lead *up to the weak*, or *through* the strong.

In second hand, your *lowest* should be played,
Unless you mean, "trump signal" to be made;
Or if you've *king and queen*, or *ace and king*,
Then one of these will be the proper thing.

Mind well the rules for *trumps*, you'll often need them:
WHEN YOU HOLD FIVE, 'TIS ALWAYS RIGHT TO LEAD THEM;
Or if the lead won't come in time to you,
Then signal to your partner so to do.

Watch also for your partner's trump request,
To which, *with less than four*, play out your *best*.

To lead through honors turned up is bad play,
Unless you want the trump suit cleared away.

When, second hand, a doubtful trick you see,
Don't trump it if you hold *more trumps than three;*
But having three or less, trump fearlessly.

When weak in trumps yourself, don't force your friend,
But always force the *adverse* strong trump hand.

For sequences, stern custom has decreed
The *lowest* you must play, if you don't lead.

When you discard, weak suit you ought to choose,
For strong ones are too valuable to lose.

WILLIAM POLE.

THE DUFFER'S WHIST MAXIMS.

"Printed for the benefit of families, and to prevent scolding."—BOB SHORT.

1. Do not confuse your mind by reading a parcel of books. Surely you've a right to play your own game, if you like. Who are the people that wrote these books? What business have they to set up their views as superior to yours? Many of these writers lay down this rule: "Lead originally from your strongest suit"; don't you do it, unless it suits your hand. It may be good in some hands, but it does n't follow that it should be in all. Lead a single card sometimes, or, at any rate, from your weakest suit, so as to make your little trumps when the suit is returned.

By following this course in leads, you will nine times out of ten ruin both your own and your partner's hands; but the tenth time you will perhaps make several little trumps, which would have been useless otherwise. In addition to this, if sometimes you lead from your strongest suit, and sometimes from your weakest, it puzzles the adversaries, and they never can tell what you have led from.

2. Seldom return your partner's lead; you have as many cards in your hand as he has it is a free country, and why should you submit to his dictation? Play the suit you deem best, without regard to any preconceived theories.

It is an excellent plan to lead out first one suit and then another. This mode of play is extremely perplexing to the whole table. If you have a fancy for books, you will find this system approved by "J. C." He says: "You mystify alike your adversaries and your partner. You turn the game upside down, reduce it to one of chance, and, in the scramble, may have as good a chance as your neighbors."

3. Especially do not return your partner's

The Duffer's Whist Maxims

lead in trumps, for not doing so now and then turns out to be advantageous. Who knows but you may make a trump by holding it up, which you certainly cannot do if your trumps are all out? Never mind the fact that you will generally lose tricks by refusing to play your partner's game.

Whenever you succeed in making a trump by your refusal, be sure to point out to your partner how fortunate it was that you played as you did.

Perhaps your partner is a much better player than you, and he may on some former occasion, with an exceptional hand, have declined to return your lead of trumps. Make a note of this. Remind him of it if he complains of your neglecting to return his lead. It is an unanswerable argument.

4. There are a lot of rules, to which, however, you need pay no attention, about leading from sequences. What can it matter which card of a sequence you lead? The sequence cards are all of the same value, and one of them is as likely to win the trick as another. Be-

sides, if you look at the books, you'll find the writers don't even know their own minds. They advise in some cases that you should lead the highest, in others the lowest, of the sequence; and in leading from ace, king, queen, they actually recommend you to begin with the middle card. Any person of common sense must infer from this that it don't matter which card of a sequence you lead.

5. There are also a number of rules about the play of the second, third, and fourth hands, but they are quite unworthy serious consideration. The exceptions are almost as numerous as the rules, so if you play by no rule at all you are about as likely to be right as wrong.

6. Before leading trumps always first get rid of all the winning cards in your plain suit. You will not then be bothered by the lead after trumps are out, and you thus shift all the responsibility of mistakes on to your partner. But if your partner has led a suit, be careful when you lead trumps to keep in your hand the best card of his lead. By this means, if he goes on with his suit, you are more likely to get the

The Duffer's Whist Maxims 127

lead after trumps are out, which, the books say, is a great advantage.

7. Take every opportunity of playing false cards, both high and low. For by deceiving all round you will now and then win an extra trick. It is often said, "Oh, but you deceive your partner." That is very true. But, then, as you have two adversaries and only one partner, it is obvious that by running dark you play two to one in your own favor. Besides this, it is very gratifying, when your trick succeeds, to have taken in your opponents, and to have won the applause of an ignorant gallery. If you play in a commonplace way, even your partner scarcely thanks you. Anybody could have done the same.

8. Whatever you do, never attend to the score, and don't watch the fall of the cards. There is no earthly reason for doing either of these. As for the score, your object is to make as many as you can. The game is five, but, if you play to score six or seven, small blame to you. Never mind running the risk of not getting another chance of making even five. Keep

as many pictures and winning cards as you can in your hand. They are pretty to look at, and if you remain with the best of each suit you effectually prevent the adversaries from bringing in a lot of small cards at the end of the hand. As to the fall of the cards, it is quite clear that it is of no use to watch them; for if everybody at the table is trying to deceive you, in accordance with Maxim 7, the less you notice the cards they play the less you will be taken in.

9. Whenever you have ruined your hand and your partner's by playing in the way here recommended, you should always say that it "made no difference."

It sometimes happens that it has made no difference, and than your excuse is clearly valid. And it will often happen that your partner does not care to argue the point with you, in which case your remark will make it clear to everybody that you have a profound insight into the game. If, however, your partner chooses to be disagreeable, and succeeds in proving you to be utterly ignorant of the first elements of whist, stick to it that you played right, that good play will sometimes turn out unfortunately, and accuse your partner of judging by results. This will generally silence him.

10. Invariably blow up your partner at the end of every hand. It is not only a most gentlemanlike employment of spare time, but it gains you the reputation of being a first-rate player.

CAVENDISH'S *Card Essays.*

WHIST, OR BUMBLEPUPPY?*

ON THINGS IN GENERAL.

" ' The time has come,' the walrus said,
' To talk of many things.' "

TO become a fair whist-player,† no wonderful attributes are required : common-sense, a small amount of knowledge,—easily acquired,—*ordinary observation of facts as they occur*, and experience, the result of that observation,—not the experience obtained by repeating the same idiotic mistakes year after year,—are about all. To save you trouble, the experience

* By permission of the author, and of G. E. Waters, London, Eng., and of Messrs. Roberts Brothers, Boston.
† Not a fine whist-player; for this is a rare bird, much more rare than a black swan (these can be bought any day at Jamrach's by the couple, but even in the present hard times when, I am informed, the markets are glutted with everything, he has not one fine whist-player in stock) : to him, in addition to common-sense and attention, genius and a thorough knowledge of Cavendish are essential.

Whist, or Bumblepuppy?

of all the best players for the last hundred years has been collected into a series of maxims, which you will find in any whist-book. These maxims you should know*; but though you know every maxim that ever was written, and are "bland, passionate, deeply religious, and also paint beautifully in water-colors," if among your other virtues the power of assimilating facts as they occur is not included, this will not avail you in the least.

Bumblepuppy—according to its own account—demands much more superfine qualities: *e. g.*, inspiration, second-sight, instinct, an intuitive perception of false cards and singletons, and an intimate acquaintance with a mysterious and Protean bogey called "the game,"—in short, everything but reason † (all these fine

* "Although these maxims may occasionally speak of things never to be done, and others always to be done, you must remember that no rules are without exception, and few more open to exceptional cases than rules for whist."—CLAY.

† Just as orthodoxy has been defined to be your own doxy, so "the game" usually means, "your own idea of the game at the time."

I have called it Protean because it assumes so many different forms (being mainly based on results), and, like the nigger's little pig, runs about to such an extent that it is impossible to get a clear view of it.

words, when boiled and peeled, turn out sometimes to mean ordinary observation, but more usually gross ignorance). So much for its theory; its practice is this:

PRACTICE OF BUMBLEPUPPY.

> "This is an anti-Christian game,
> Unlawful both in thing and name."—*Hudibras.*

(1) Lead a singleton whenever you have one.

(2) With two small trumps and no winning card, lead a trump.

(3) Ruff a suit of which your partner clearly holds the best, if you are weak in trumps.

(4) Never ruff anything if you are strong.

(5) Never return your partner's trump if you can possibly avoid it, unless he manifestly led it to bring in a suit of which you led a singleton.

(6) Deceive him whenever you get a chance.

(7) Open a new suit every time you have the lead.

(8) Never pay any attention to your partner's first discard, unless it is a forced discard. Lead your own suit.

(9) Never force him under any circumstances unless you hold at least five trumps with two honors; even if you lose the rubber by it, play "the game!"

(10) Devote all your remaining energies to looking for a signal in the last trick. If you are unable to discover which was your partner's card,—after keeping the table waiting for two minutes,—lead him a trump on suspicion.

Play all your cards alike, without emphasis or hesitation; how can you expect your partner to have any confidence in your play when it is evident to him from your hesitation that you have no confidence in it yourself?

If your partner renounces, and you think fit to inquire whether he is void of the suit, do so quietly; don't offer a hint for his future guidance by glaring or yelling at him.

Don't ask idiotic questions. If you led an ace, and the two, three, and four are played to the trick, what is the use of asking your partner to draw his card? If you hold all the remaining cards of a suit, why inquire whether he has any?

Don't talk in the middle of the hand.* However you may be tempted to use bad language,—and I must admit the temptation is often very great,—always recollect that though your Latin grammar says "*humanum est irasci*," the antidote grows near the bane; for—at the bottom of the very preceding page—it also says "*pii orant taciti.*"

"'T is best sometimes your censure to restrain."
POPE.

The wisest man who ever lived says: "He that holdeth his peace is counted wise, and he that shutteth his lips is esteemed a man of understanding." Such a reputation appears cheap

---

* "Though 'whist' is reported to be an old English word meaning 'silence,' and though it is advisable for many reasons that it should be played with reasonable quiet, it is not at all compulsory to conduct yourself as if in the monastery of La Trappe: you have a perfect right—as far as the laws of whist are concerned—to discuss at any time the price of stocks, the latest scandal, or even the play going on, 'provided that no intimation whatever, by word or gesture be given as to the state of your own hand or the game.'"—*Etiquette of Whist.*

At bumblepuppy you had better waive this right altogether; for if under any circumstances you open your mouth, you will infallibly put your foot into it.

Whist, or Bumblepuppy?

at the price; but if you are of the opinion of J. P. Robinson, that "they did n't know everything down in Judee," you can call your partner any names you like as soon as the hand is over.* You need not be at all particular what for; any crime of omission or commission—real or fancied—will do. If, after the game is over, you discover that it might have been saved or won by doing something different, however idiotic, grumble at him.†

---

* "Avoid playing with those who instruct, or rather find fault, while the hand is playing. They are generally unqualified by ignorance, and judge from consequences; but, if not, advice while playing does more harm than good."—MATHEWS.

"The empty vessel makes the greatest sound."—SHAKESPEARE

"Talking over the hand *after* it has been played is not uncommonly called a bad habit and an annoyance: I am firmly persuaded it is one of the readiest ways of learning whist."—CLAY.

† "'O dreary life!' we cry, 'O dreary life!'
   And still the generations of the birds
   Sing through our sighing, and the flocks and herds
   Serenely live while we are keeping strife."

"The education of the whist-player is peculiar. How he becomes a whist-player, nobody knows. He never learns his alphabet or the catechism, or anything that he ought to do. He appears full-grown, mushroom-like. He remembers some one blowing him up for doing something he ought not to have done, and somebody else blowing him up for not doing something else; and

It is quite legitimate to revile him for not playing cards he never held : if he should have the temerity to point out that the facts are against you, revile the facts.

If there is really a diabolical mistake in the case, and you happen to have made it yourself, revile him with additional ferocity.

Failing any other grievance, you can always prove to demonstration—and at interminable length—that if his cards, or your cards, or both he is blown up to the end of the chapter. This phase of being blown up is varied by grumbling, sometimes aloud, sometimes *sotto voce;* so that the whist-player is reared on scolding and grumbling as other youngsters are reared on pap. Truly this is a happy life. Some men grumble on principle because it is a national privilege, and they avail themselves of the Englishman's birthright.

> ' A sect whose chief devotion lies
> In odd perverse antipathies ;
> In falling out with that or this,
> And finding somewhat still amiss ;
> More peevish, cross, and splenetic
> Than dog distract, or monkey sick.'—*Hudibras.*

Some do it because they believe, that, if they grumble enough, it will bring them luck. Some do it in the hope that they will excite sympathy, and that their friends will feel for their ill-fortune, which, by-the-by, whist-players never do. Some grumble to annoy their friends, and we are bound to say these succeed."—*Westminster Papers.*

> " The croaking nuisance lurked in every nook ;
>   And the land stank—so numerous was the fry."
>   COWPER.

your cards, had been just the reverse of what they were, the result would have been different. This certainly opens a wide field for speculation ; but it is neither an instructive nor entertaining amusement, though it kills time.

There is a theory, which, according to some evil-disposed persons, may easily be made too much of,—the injury to yourself being remote and doubtful, while the gratification of annoying him is certain and immediate,—that abusing your partner, as having a tendency to make him play worse, is a mistake from a pecuniary point of view. Of course it is a mistake, but not for such a paltry reason as that : take a higher standpoint ! Whether you are winning or losing,—

> " You should *never* let
> Your angry passions rise."—WATTS.

Don't cry !

> " Ill betides a nation when
> She sees the tears of bearded men."

And you will have a beard yourself some time, if you don't lead the penultimate of five. Without exciting the slightest sympathy on the part of an unfeeling public, crying deranges the other secretions. The Laureate says, tears are idle, and professes ignorance of their meaning: if he played whist, he would know that they injure the cards and make them sticky.

Don't play out of your turn, nor draw your card before that turn comes.

Don't ride a hobby to death! *In ordinary whist* three prevailing hobbies are so cruelly over-ridden that I am surprised the active and energetic Mr. Colam has never interfered: these are:

(1) The penultimate of a long suit;

(2) The signal for trumps;

(3) Not forcing your partner unless you are strong in trumps—under any circumstances.

The first is nothing but a nuisance.* The second is stated to simplify the game, and to cause greater attention to be paid to it: prac-

---

* "They are intent on some wretched crotchet like the lowest but one."

"Every time he can lead a lowest but one, no matter what the state of the game or the score, that lead he is sure to make; and we believe there are some neophytes who would lose their money with pleasure if they could only tell their partners afterwards that they had led the lowest but one."—*Westminster Papers.*

tically the entire time of the players is taken up either in devising absurd signals, or in looking for and failing to see them. The third is responsible for losing about as many games as anything I am acquainted with, though the constant and aimless changing of suits runs it close.

Is it any reason—because you have no trumps—that you should announce that circumstance early in the hand to the general public, and prevent your partner making one? If he has them all, you cannot injure him; if he has not, the adversaries will play through him and strangle him: how is it that you are afraid to let your partner make a certain trick, but you are never afraid to open a new suit?

There is an impression abroad that there is a law of whist somewhere to this effect: "Never force your partner at any stage of the game unless you yourself are strong in trumps."

Let us see what the authorities say on the point:

"Keep in mind that general maxims pre-suppose the game and hand at their commencement, and that material changes in them frequently require that a different mode of play should be adopted."

"It is a general maxim not to force your partner unless strong in trumps yourself. There are, however, many exceptions to this rule, as:

"(1) If your partner has led a single card;

"(2) If it saves or wins a particular point;

"(3) If great strength in trumps is declared against you;

"(4) If you have a probability of a saw;

"(5) If your partner has been forced, and did not lead trumps;

"(6) It is often right in playing for an odd trick;

"If your partner shows a weak game, force him whether or not you are otherwise entitled to do it."— MATHEWS.

With a weak trump hand, force your partner:

"(1) When he has already shown a desire to be forced or weakness in trumps;

"(2) When you have a cross ruff;

"(3) When you are playing a close game, as for the odd trick, and often when one trick saves or wins the game or a point;

"(4) When great strength in trumps has been declared against you."—CAVENDISH.

"Do not force your partner unless to make sure of the tricks required to save or win the game;

"Or unless he has been already forced, and has not led a trump;

"Or unless he has asked to be forced by leading from a single card, or two weak cards;

"Or unless the adversary has led, or asked for trumps."
—CLAY.

"Unless your partner has shown great strength in trumps, or a wish to get them drawn, or has refused to ruff a doubtful card, give him the option of making a small trump; unless you have some good reason for not doing so, other than a weak suit of trumps in your own hand."—*Art of Practical Whist.*

With these extracts before you, perhaps you will dismiss from your mind the popular fallacy that you are under any compulsion to lose the game because your trumps are not quite so strong as you could wish.

Make a note of this.

Maxims were not invented for the purpose of preventing you from either saving or winning the game, though it is their unfortunate fate to be epitomized and perverted out of all reasonable shape. The ill-advised dictum, "Suppose the adversaries are four, and you, with the lead, have a bad hand: the best play is in defiance of all system, to lead out your best trump," was comparatively innocuous, till some ingenious person, with a turn for abbreviation, altered it into, "Whenever you hold nothing, lead a trump!" Use your common-sense.*

* "Common-sense (which in truth is very uncommon) is the best sense I know of. Abide by it: it will counsel you best."—*Chesterfield Letters.*

I have gone into this matter at considerable length, because I am convinced that however many people, once affluent, are now in misery and want, owing to their not having led trumps with five,—Clay gave the number as eleven thousand,—a far larger number have been reduced to this deplorable condition by changing suits, and refusing *on principle* to save the game by forcing their partner.

Before quitting the subject, there is another branch of it worthy of a little consideration. When your partner has shown by his discard which is his suit, and you hold two or three small cards in it, however strong you may be in trumps,—*unless everything depends on one trick*,—do you expect to gain much by forcing him and making yourself third player? Though it is usual to play in this absurd way, is there any objection to first playing his suit, and—as, *ex hypothesi*, you are strong in trumps—forcing him afterwards?

Play always as simply and intelligibly as you

can.* Never think! † Know! Leave thinking to the Teuton.

> "A Briton knows; or, if he knows it not,
> He ought."—COWPER.

After the game has begun, the time for thinking has passed: as soon as a card is led, it is the time for action, the time to bring your previously acquired knowledge to bear.

P. S.—When pointing out your rights, I omitted to state, that, before you proceed to give your partner a piece of your mind, you should always call your honors; for by neglecting this simple precaution you will often lay yourself open to a crushing rejoinder.—*Experto crede.*

---

* In addition to your partner not being able to see your cards—in itself a disadvantage—he is, by an immutable law of nature, much inferior in perception to yourself: you should bear this in mind, and not be too hard on the poor fellow.

† This is at first sight rather an appalling proposition, but the advice I give you I have always endeavored to follow myself; and I am not a solitary case, for in *The Nineteenth Century Review* for May, 1879, I find the writer of one of the articles in the same boat. This thoughtful writer—he must have been thoughtful, otherwise his lucubration would not have been accepted—says, "I have given up the practice of thinking, or may be I never had it."

THINKING.

"With some unmeaning thing, that they call thought."
PQPE.

Never think!

Unless you have some remarkably good reason for taking your own course, do as you are told. If your partner leads you a small trump, return it at once.

"Gratia ab officio, quod mora tardat, abest."

This is a much more simple and satisfactory plan than to proceed to think that he may have no more, or that the fourth player must hold major tenace. No one will admit more readily than I do, that you are much the better player of the two, still allow him to have some idea of the state of your own hand.

Don't think, whenever you see a card played, that it is necessarily false: as, on the whole, true cards are in the majority, you are rather more likely to be wrong than right, and the betting must be against you in the long-run.

"My business and your own is not to inquire
Into such matters, but to mind our cue,—
Which is to act as we are bid to do."—BYRON.

If you are blessed with a sufficiently sharp eye to the left, you may occasionally *know* that a card is false; but I should not describe knowledge acquired in that way as thinking, I should use quite a different expression.

With the military gentleman who anathematized intellect, I deeply sympathize. Profound thought about facts which have just taken place under your own eye is the bane of whist.

Why imitate Mark Twain's fiery steed? Why, when it is your business to go on, "lean your head against something, and think"?

Whether you have seen a thing, or not seen it, there can be no necessity for thought. Recondite questions—such as whether the seven is the best of a suit of which all the others but the six are out, or whether a card is the twelfth or thirteenth—can be answered by a rational being in two ways, and two only: either he knows, or he does not know; there is no *tertium quid*. The curious practice of gazing intently at the chandelier, and looking as intelligent as nature will permit,—if not more so,—though it is less confusing than going to the last trick for information, and imposes upon some people, is no answer at all*: this, in whist circles, is called, or miscalled *thinking*. It is not a new invention, for it has been known and practised from the earliest times. "There is a generation, oh, how lofty are their eyes! and their eye-lids are lifted up" (Prov. xxx., 13, B.C. 1,000). Pecksniff, who had an extensive acquaintance with the weaknesses of human nature, knew it: you, and all other schoolboys, are adepts at it.

In Greek the very name of man—$\overset{\text{'}}{\alpha}\nu\theta\rho\omega\pi o\varsigma$—was derived from this peculiar method of feigning intelligence, and it was by no means unknown to the Romans.

> " Pronaque cum spectent animalia cœtera terram,
> Os homini sublime dedit cœlumque tueri."

But, however ancient and venerable the practice may be, it is one of those numerous practices more honored in the breach than in the observance. Surely looking at the table is more in accordance with the dictates of common-

---

* Making passes in the air with your hand, as if you were about to mesmerize the table, is another favorite stratagem.

sense than attempting to eliminate unknown quantities from a chandelier. In the one you have gas, and probably water: on the other,— lying open before you,—the data required. I have now endeavored, not to teach you either whist or bumblepuppy, but to point out a few of the differences between them, and to start you on the right road. The first is a game of reason and common-sense, played in combination with your partner; the second is a game of inspiration, hap-hazard, and absurdity, where your partner is your deadliest enemy. I have made a few extracts from Mathews: partly because I don't like novelties merely because they are novelties; partly to convince the bumblepuppist (if anything will convince him) that when he tells me the recognized play is a new invention, introduced by Cavendish for his especial annoyance, he does not know what he is talking about; and partly to show you that since that book was written—eighty years ago—the main principles of whist are almost unaltered.

The chapter on etiquette is since his time; but, though the game has been cut down one-half, take away from Mathews his slight partiality for sneakers (to be accounted for by the possibility of his partner at that remote period being even a more dangerous lunatic than yours is at present, and the consequent necessity of playing more on the defensive; for leading singletons, whatever else it may do, does not injure the leader),* take away from the play of to-day its signal, its echo, and its penultimate of a long suit,—all excrescences of doubtful advantage for general purposes, and the last two more adapted to that antediluvian epoch when human life was longer,—and the continuity of the game is clear.† Whether whist would gain anything by their omission, I am unable to say.

---

* The difference here is more apparent than real: Mathews, with considerable limitations, advocates leading singletons. Nowadays the practice is decried; but I regret to say, that, as far as my experience goes, the principal obstacle to leading a singleton is not having a singleton to lead.

† " We suspect that Cavendish very often must have objected to that ancient plagiarist Mathews for stealing his ideas."
"If their ideas are not identical, it is rather difficult to find where the one begins, and the other ends."—*Westminster Papers*.
" I contend that there is no essential difference between modern and old-fashioned whist; *i.e*, between Hoyle and Cavendish, Mathews and J. C."—MOGUL.

Whist, or Bumblepuppy?

The attention, now always on the strain in *looking* for its accidents, would have a spare moment or two to devote to its essentials: whether it would do anything of the kind, is another matter.

Those followers of Darwin and believers in the doctrine of evolution, to whom it is a source of comfort that an ascidian monad and not Eve was their first parent, must find the whist-table rather a stumbling-block: they will see there uncommonly few specimens of the survival of the fittest.

The philosopher of Chelsea long since arrived at the unsatisfactory and sweeping conclusion, that the population of these islands are mostly fools; and he has made no exception for the votaries of whist. Still, it has the reputation of being a very pretty game, though this reputation must be based to a great extent on conjecture; for apart from its other little peculiarities,—on some of which I have briefly touched,—its features are so fearfully disfigured by bumblepuppy, that it is as difficult to give a positive opinion as to say whether a woman suffering from malignant small-pox might or might not be good-looking under happier circumstances. The sublime self-confidence expressed in the distich,—

> " When I see thee as thou art,
> I'll praise thee as I ought,"—

has not been vouchsafed to me; but if ever I obtain a clear view of it, I will undertake to report upon it to the best of my ability.

You may have heard, that if you are ignorant of whist you are preparing for yourself a miserable old age: it is by no means certain that a knowledge of it—as practised at this particular epoch—is to be classed with the beatitudes.

THE DOMESTIC RUBBER.

A third variety of whist, the domestic rubber, I have passed over in silence. What takes place in the sanctity of private life, it would be as unbecoming for me to divulge as for you to seek to know.

> " O'er all its faults we draw a tender veil,
> So great its sorrows, and so sad its tale."

Whist, or Bumblepuppy? 151

At the same time I don't think I am violating any confidence in stating that you will neither find there signalling, nor the penultimate of five and its developments: yet, though free from these annoyances, the game, even when mitigated by muffins, music, and the humanizing influence of woman, is inexpressibly dreary, and you had better keep out of it if you can; but should this not be practicable,—for some relative from whom you have a reasonable expectation of a tip may be staying in the house, and you may be compelled to sacrifice yourself either on the altar of duty or of self-interest,—then never forget that sweetness of temper is much more important here than knowledge of whist, and, consoling yourself with the two following reflections —

(1) That (according to Epicurus) prolonged pain is rather pleasant than otherwise, extreme pain always short*;

(2) That those whom the gods love die young—

---

* He is right to some extent: the domestic rubber always closes early.

when your hour arrives, bare your throat to the knife with a smile.

So shall your memory smell sweet and blossom in domestic circles.

"Pembridge."

CARDS SPIRITUALIZED.

THE following curious article is taken from an English newspaper of the year 1773, and is there called the "Perpetual Almanack; or, Soldier's Prayer Book," by Richard Lane, a private soldier, belonging to the 42d regiment, who was taken before the Mayor of Glasgow for playing cards during divine service.

The sergeant commanded the soldiers to church, and when the parson read his prayers and took his text, those who had a Bible took it out; but this soldier had neither a Bible nor a common prayer-book; but pulling out a pack of cards, he spread them out before him. He first looked at one card and then at another. The sergeant of the company saw him and said:

"Richard put up the cards; this is no place for them."

"Never mind that," said Richard.

When the service was over, the constable took Richard prisoner and brought him before the Mayor.

"Well," said the Mayor, "What have you brought this soldier here for?"

"For playing cards in church."

"Well, soldier, what have you to say for yourself?"

"Much, sir, I hope."

"Very good; if not I will punish you more than ever man was punished."

"I have been," said the soldier, "about six weeks on the march; I have neither Bible nor common prayer-book; I have nothing but a common pack of cards, and I hope to satisfy your worship of the purity of my intentions."

"Very good," said the Mayor.

Then, spreading the cards before the Mayor, he began with the ace:

"When I see the ace, it reminds me there is but one God.

"When I see the deuce, it reminds me of Father and Son.

"When I see the tray, it reminds me of Father, Son, and Holy Ghost.

"When I see the four, it reminds me of the four evangelists that preached, viz., Matthew, Mark, Luke, and John.

"When I see the five, it reminds me of the five wise virgins that trimmed their lamps. There were ten, but five were fools, and were sent out.

"When I see the six, it reminds me that in six days the Lord made heaven and earth.

"When I see the seven, it reminds me that on the seventh day God rested from the works He had made, and hallowed it.

"When I see the eight, it reminds me of the eight righteous persons that were saved when God drowned the world, viz., Noah and his wife, his three sons and their wives.

"When I see the nine, it reminds me of the nine lepers that were cleansed by our Saviour. There were ten, but nine never returned thanks.

"When I see the ten, it reminds me of the ten commandments, which God handed down to Moses on a table of stone.

"When I see the king, it reminds me of the great King of Heaven, which is God Almighty.

"When I see the queen, it reminds me of the Queen of Sheba, who went to hear the wisdom of Solomon, for she was as wise a woman as he a man. She brought with her fifty boys and fifty girls, all dressed in boy's apparel, for King Solomon to tell which were girls. King Solomon sent for water for them to wash themselves; the girls washed to the elbows, and the boys only to the wrists—so King Solomon told by this."

"Well," said the Mayor, "you have given a description of every card in the pack except one."

"What is that?" asked the soldier.

"The knave," said the Mayor.

"I will give your honor a description of that, too, if you will not be angry."

"I will not," said the Mayor, "if you will not term me to be a knave."

"Well," said the soldier, "the greatest knave that I know of is the constable who brought me here."

"I do not know," said the Mayor, "whether he is the greatest knave, but I know he's the greatest fool."

"When I count how many spots in a pack, I find three hundred and sixty-five—as many as there are days in a year.

"When I count the number of cards in a pack, I find there are fifty-two—as many weeks as there are in a year; and I find four suits—the number of weeks in the month.

"I find there are twelve picture cards in the pack, representing the number of months in the year; and counting the tricks, I find thirteen—the number of weeks in a quarter.

"So you see, sir, the pack of cards serves for a Bible, almanac, and common prayer-book to me."

ANONYMOUS.

MRS. BATTLE'S OPINIONS ON WHIST.

"A CLEAR fire, a clean hearth, and the rigor of the game." This was the celebrated *wish* of old Sarah Battle (now with God), who, next to her devotions, loved a good game of whist. She was none of your lukewarm gamesters, your half-and-half players, who have no objection to take a hand, if you want one to make up a rubber; who affirm that they have no pleasure in winning; that they like to win one game and lose another; that they can while away an hour very agreeably at a card-table, but are indifferent whether they play or no; and will desire an adversary, who has slipped a wrong card, to take it up and play another. These insufferable triflers are the curse of a table. One of these flies will spoil a whole pot. Of such it may be said that they do not play at cards, but only play at playing at them.

Sarah Battle was none of that breed. She detested them, as I do, from her heart and soul, and would not, save upon a striking emergency, willingly seat herself at the same table with them. She loved a thorough-paced partner, a determined enemy. She took, and gave, no concessions. She hated favors. She never made a revoke, nor even passed it over in her adversary without exacting the utmost forfeiture. She fought a good fight—cut and thrust. She held not her good sword (her cards) "like a dancer." She sate bolt upright, and neither showed you her cards, nor desired to see yours. All people have their blind side—their superstitions ; and I have heard her declare, under the rose, that Hearts was her favorite suit.

I never in my life—and I knew Sarah Battle many of the best years of it—saw her take out her snuff-box when it was her turn to play, or snuff a candle in the middle of a game, or ring for a servant till it was fairly over. She never introduced or connived at miscellaneous conversation during its progress. As she emphatically observed, "cards were cards"; and if I ever saw unmingled distaste in her fine last-century countenance, it was at the airs of a young gentleman of a literary turn, who had been with difficulty persuaded to take a hand, and who, in his excess of candor, declared that he thought there was no harm in unbending the mind now and then, after serious studies, in recreations of that kind! She could not bear to have her noble occupation, to which she wound up her faculties, considered in that light. It was her business, her duty, the thing she came into the world to do,—and she did it. She unbent her mind afterwards over a book.

Pope was her favorite author; his *Rape of the Lock* her favorite work. She once did me the honor to play over with me (with the cards) his celebrated game of ombre in that poem; and to explain to me how far it agreed with, and in what points it would be found to differ from, tradrille. Her illustrations were apposite and poignant; and I have had the pleasure of sending the substance of them to Mr. Bowles; but I suppose they came too late to be inserted among his ingenious notes upon that author.

Quadrille, she has often told me, was her first love; but whist had engaged her maturer esteem. The former, she said, was showy and specious, and likely to allure young persons. The uncertainty and quick shifting of partners —a thing which the constancy of whist abhors —the dazzling supremacy and regal investiture of spadille—absurd, as she justly observed, in the pure aristocracy of whist, where his crown and garter give him no proper power above his brother nobility of the aces;—the giddy vanity, so taking to the inexperienced, of playing alone; above all, the overpowering attractions of a *Sans Prendre Vole*,—to the triumph of which there is certainly nothing parallel or approaching, in the contingencies of whist;—all these, she would say, make quadrille a game of captivation to the young and enthusiastic. But whist was the *solider* game—that was her word. It was a long meal: not like quadrille a feast of snatches. One or two rubbers might coëxtend in duration with an evening. They gave time to form rooted friendships, to cultivate steady enmities. She despised the chance-started, capricious, and ever-fluctuating alliances of the other. The skirmishes of quadrille, she would say, reminded her of the petty ephemeral embroilments of the little Italian states, depicted by Machiavel, perpetually changing postures and connection; bitter foes to-day, sugared darlings to-morrow; kissing and scratching in a breath;—but the wars of whist were comparable to the long, steady, deep-rooted, national antipathies of the great French and English nations.

A grave simplicity was what she chiefly admired in her favorite game. There was nothing silly in it, like the nob in cribbage—nothing superfluous. No *flushes*—that most irrational of all pleas that a reasonable being can set up;—that any one should claim four by virtue of holding cards of the same mark and color, without reference to the playing of the game, or the individual worth or pretensions of the cards themselves! She held this to be a solecism; as pitiful an ambition in cards as alliteration is in authorship. She despised superficiality, and looked deeper than the colors of things. Suits were soldiers, she would say, and must have a uniformity of array to distinguish them; but what should we say to a foolish squire, who should claim a merit from dressing up his tenantry in red jackets, that never were to be marshalled—never to take the field? She even wished that whist were more simple than it is; and, in my mind, would have stripped it of some appendages, which in the state of human frailty, may be venially, and even commendably, allowed of. She saw no reason for the deciding of the trump by the turn of the card. Why not one suit always trumps? Why two colors when the mark of the suits would have sufficiently distinguished them without it?

"But the eye, my dear Madam, is agreeably refreshed with the variety. Man is not a creature of pure reason—he must have his senses delightfully appealed to. We see it in Roman Catholic countries, where the music and the paintings draw in many to worship, whom your Quaker spirit of unsensualizing would have kept out. You yourself have a pretty collection of paintings,—but confess to me, whether, walking in your gallery at Sandham, among those clear Vandykes, or among the Paul Potters in the anteroom, you ever felt your bosom glow with an elegant delight, at all comparable to *that* you have it in your power to experience most evenings over a well-arranged assortment of the court-cards?—the pretty antic habits, like heralds in a procession—the gay triumph-assuring scarlets—the contrasting deadly-killing sables—the 'hoary majesty of spades'—Pam in all his glory!

"All these might be dispensed with; and with their naked names upon the drab pasteboard, the game might go on very well, pictureless. But the *beauty* of cards would be extinguished forever. Stripped of all that is imaginative in them, they must degenerate into mere gambling. Imagine a dull deal board, or drum-head, to spread them on, instead of that nice verdant carpet (next to Nature's), fittest arena for those courtly combatants to play their gallant jousts and tourneys in! Exchange those delicately-turned ivory markers —(work of Chinese artists, unconscious of their symbol, or as profanely slighting their true application as the arrantest Ephesian journeyman that turned out those little shrines for the goddess)—exchange them for little bits of leather (our ancestors' money), or chalk and a slate!"

The old lady, with a smile, confessed the soundness of my logic; and to her approbation of my arguments on her favorite topic that evening, I have always fancied myself indebted for the legacy of a curious cribbage-board, made of the finest Sienna marble, which her maternal uncle (old Walter Plumer, whom I have elsewhere celebrated), brought with him from Florence;—this, and a trifle of five hundred pounds, came to me at her death.

The former bequest (which I do not least value) I have kept with religious care; though she herself, to confess a truth, was never greatly taken with cribbage. It was an essentially vulgar game, I have heard her say,—disputing with her uncle, who was very partial to it. She could never heartily bring her mouth to pronounce "*Go*"—or "*That's a go.*" She called it an ungrammatical game. The pegging teased her. I once knew her to forfeit a rubber (a five-dollar stake), because she would not take advantage of the turn-up knave, which would have given it her, but which she must have claimed by the disgraceful tenure of declaring "*two for his heels.*" There is something extremely genteel in this sort of self-denial. Sarah Battle was a gentlewoman born.

Piquet she held the best game at the cards for two persons, though she would ridicule the pedantry of the terms,—such as pique—repique—the capot,—they savored (she thought) of affectation. But games for two, or even three, she never greatly cared for. She loved the quadrate, or square. She would argue thus: Cards are warfare; the ends are gain, with glory. But cards are war, in disguise of a sport; when single adversaries encounter, the ends proposed are too palpable. By themselves, it is too close a fight; with spectators, it is not much bettered. No looker-on can be interested, except for a bet, and then it is a mere affair of money; he cares not for your luck *sympathetically*, or for your play. Three are still worse; a mere naked war of every man against every man, as in cribbage, without league or alliance; or a rotation of petty and contradictory interests, a succession of heartless leagues, and not much more hearty infractions of them, as in tradrille. But in square games (*she meant whist*), all that is possible to be attained in card-playing is accomplished. There are the incentives of profit with honor, common to every species,—though the *latter* can be but very imperfectly enjoyed in those other games, where the spectator is only feebly a participator. But the parties in whist are spectators and principals too. They are a theatre to themselves, and a looker-on is not wanted. He is rather worse than nothing, and an impertinence. Whist abhors neutrality, or interests beyond its sphere. You glory in some surprising stroke of skill or fortune, not because a cold—or even an interested—bystander witnesses it, but because your *partner* sympathizes in the contingency. You win for two. You triumph for two. Two are exalted. Two again are mortified; which divides their disgrace, as the conjunction doubles (by taking off the invidiousness) your glories. Two losing to two are better reconciled, than one to one in that close butchery. The hostile feeling is weakened by multiplying the channels. War has become a civil game. By such reasonings as these the old lady was accustomed to defend her favorite pastime.

No inducement could ever prevail upon her to play at any game, where chance entered into the composition, *for nothing*. Chance, she would argue,—and here again, admire the subtlety of her conclusion,—chance is nothing, but where something else depends upon it. It is obvious that cannot be *glory*. What rational cause of exultation could it give to a man to turn up size ace a hundred times together by himself? or before spectators, where no stake was depending? Make a lottery of a hundred thousand tickets with but one fortunate number, and what possible principle of our nature, except stupid wonderment, could it gratify to gain that number as many times successively, without a prize? Therefore she disliked the mixture of chance in backgammon, where it was not played for money. She called it foolish, and those people idiots who were taken with a lucky hit under such circumstances. Games of pure skill were as little to her fancy. Played for a stake, they were a mere system of overreaching. Played for glory, they were a mere setting of one man's wit,—his memory, or combination-faculty rather—against another's; like a mock engagement at a review, bloodless and profitless. She could not conceive a *game* wanting the spritely infusion of chance, the handsome excuses of good fortune. Two people playing at chess in a corner of a room, whilst whist was stirring in the centre, would inspire her with insufferable horror and *ennui*. Those well-cut similitudes of Castles and

Knights, the *imagery* of the board, she would argue (and I think in this case justly) were entirely misplaced and senseless. Those hard head-contests can in no instance ally with the fancy. They reject form and color. A pencil and dry slate (she used to say) were the proper arena for such combatants.

To those puny objectors against cards, as nurturing the bad passions, she would retort, that man is a gaming animal. He must be always trying to get the better in something or other;—that this passion can scarcely be more safely expended than upon a game at cards; that cards are a temporary illusion;—in truth, a mere drama; for we do but *play* at being mightily concerned, where a few idle shillings are at stake, yet, during the illusion, we *are* as mightily concerned as those whose stake is crowns and kingdoms. They are a sort of dream-fighting; much ado; great battling and little bloodshed; mighty means for disproportioned ends; quite as diverting, and a great deal more innoxious, than many of those more serious *games* of life which men play, without esteeming them to be such.

With great deference to the old lady's judgment in these matters, I think I have experienced some moments in my life, when playing at cards *for nothing* has even been agreeable. When I am in sickness, or not in the best spirits, I sometimes call for the cards, and play a game at piquet *for love* with my cousin Bridget—Bridget Elia.

I grant there is something sneaking in it; but with a toothache, or a sprained ankle,—when you are subdued and humble,—you are glad to put up with an inferior spring of action.

There is such a thing in nature, I am convinced, as *sick whist*.

I grant it is not the highest style of man—I deprecate the *manes* of Sarah Battle—she lives not, alas! to whom I should apologize.

At such times, those *terms*, which my old friend objected to, come in as something admissible. I love to get a tierce or a quatorze, though they mean nothing. I am subdued to an inferior interest. Those shadows of winning amuse me.

That last game I had with my sweet cousin (I capotted her)—(dare I tell thee, how foolish

I am?)—I wished it might have lasted forever, though we gained nothing, and lost nothing; though it was a mere shade of play, I would be content to go on in that idle folly forever. The pipkin should be ever boiling, that was to prepare the gentle lenitive to my foot, which Bridget was doomed to apply after the game was over; and, as I do not much relish appliances, there it should ever bubble. Bridget and I should be ever playing.

CHARLES LAMB.

LADIES' WHIST.

NOT many years ago there came from America a treatise upon whist, containing certain theories which were the subject of hot debate among our whist-players at home, and which are still known and referred to as "American leads." The latest ideas that have been contributed by the United States on the subject of the game are hardly so useful or worthy of discussion; but as they throw a curious and unexpected light upon a game played by ladies—which is not whist, although they call it by that name—we are unwilling to let them pass altogether in silence. It would appear from the American papers that the ladies of New York have decided that whist is an excellent opportunity for displaying the charms of their persons, and are become so enamored of the game in consequence, that there is a most unusual and fashionable demand among them for professors of the art—an art which, in their case, can not be learnt from any treatises that are extant; for neither does the ancient Hoyle nor the more modern Cavendish say a word about the elegances of whist-playing, or the airs and graces to be practised by the players. Their professors are required to teach them, not how to play a hand, but how to display a pretty hand and arm to the greatest advantage; a suit of diamonds is not more necessary in the pack than a suit of diamonds upon their fingers; and the privilege of dealing ranks second to that of shuffling the cards. They require a professor to teach them whist in the same way as Mr. Turveydrop, late lamented professor of deportment, would have taught them to play lawn tennis. In fact, his art is merely supplementary to that of another American professor,— the *Manicure*. This latest development of whist-playing is not likely to add to the science of the game; but,

Ladies' Whist

as it throws a curious side-light upon "ladies' whist" in general, it is worthy of consideration.

What we call "ladies' whist," what Charles Lamb called "sick whist," and what we have heard an elderly and morose whist-player describe as "bumblepuppy"—a word with a dark but suggestive meaning—are all practically the same game,—a very pleasant game, but not whist in the strictest sense of the word. We would not suggest that ladies cannot play the strict game; on the contrary, some of them play it remarkably well,—witness the celebrated Sarah Battle, for instance. But it cannot be denied that the average lady whist-player is addicted to play that is rather peculiar than scientific. We need not make mention of those dear ladies who, on sitting down at the whist-table, propound such riddles as—"How many cards do you deal to each person?" or "Does a king count more than an ace?"—for they are outside the pale; but we will content ourselves with speaking of the average player, and by these signs we may know her.

She will invariably try to cheat in cutting

for partners, for she cannot bear to leave so important a choice to be decided by chance. In dealing, she will begin with the greatest care and deliberation, but suddenly there will occur to her mind a story, which, with much animation, she will proceed to relate until the trump is turned up in the wrong place. She can never be persuaded that she has misdealt until the cards have been carefully counted at least three times. Another time she will beg her partner to deal for her, and overwhelm him with reproachful glances should he turn up a small card for the trump. It is easy to know whether she has taken up a good or an indifferent hand; if it be a good one, she never tires of contemplating it, will arrange and re-arrange it a hundred times, while she fingers with ill-concealed impatience the card that she wishes to play; if it looks but an indifferent one, she, too, will assume an air of indifference, will gaze with an abstracted look into the farther corners of the room, and drum upon the table with the fingers of one hand while the other holds the cards carelessly shut up in a pack. If she has five trumps in her hand, she will not lead them,—no, nothing will induce her to lead them, not even if her partner has called for them. He is ill-advised if he remonstrates with her afterwards. She looks at him with the sweetest wonder in her eyes, as she protests that she never *heard* him. *En revanche*, in the course of the next game she will trump his best card, and gather up the trick with a beaming smile of genial triumph. To do her justice, she does not often revoke; when she does revoke, she discovers her offence with the prettiest air of defiance imaginable, and at least ten minutes' discussion, combined with the display of all the back tricks, are needed before it can be proved to her satisfaction,—even then she has a great deal to say, and leaves it to be finally understood that not she herself, but her partner, has been most to blame in this matter. Indeed, he is fortunate if the matter is allowed to rest then, and if he is not subjected to a spirited homily on the misleading nature of his play. She loves, above all things, to make what she calls a good trick,—that is to say, a trick with lots of court cards in it. If the two of spades be led, followed by the four, she will play a knave, even though she has the ace in hand, because she cannot bear to waste the latter upon two such insignificant cards; and it is with feelings of unbounded indignation that she sees the trick fall to the queen of the fourth hand. The feelings of her partner who led from a king need not be described, because his feelings, of course, are not worth mentioning. She also loves to score by honors, but she cannot endure that her adversaries should hold them; if they do so too often, she will have grave doubts as to the advisability of counting honors at all, and will give vent to some very serious reflections upon the relative value of good hands and good play, of blind chance and science. The simple rules of scoring she can never master; she generally requests her partner to mark the score, but that does not prevent her from challenging the correctness of the result, should it not be in her favor. Of all her propensities, the most curious, the most ineradicable, is the one that prompts her to hoard her trumps.

Nothing, as we have already said, can induce her to lead them. She prefers to save them up as a kind of *bonne bouche*, a display of fireworks for the end of the game. She looks upon them as things that are too precious for use; she regards them with a superstitious reverence. Should her partner lead them, "What? trumps!" she exclaims in a tone of pained surprise at his wasteful audacity; she will play her card grudgingly, and take the trick perhaps, but she will not return his lead,—no, she cannot bring herself to return his lead. There was an eminent whist-player, of whom it was related that, whenever he found himself seated at the whist-table with ladies, he used to tell them the following tale as a kind of prologue to the game: "I once knew a lady who held five trumps in her hand, and who failed to lead them. She ended sadly";—and here his voice sank to an impressive whisper—"she died in the workhouse." Whether or not this precautionary measure was attended with success tradition does not say; we should be inclined to doubt its efficacy. But to sum up our lady whist-player: she is delightful, she is charming, she is everything that is good and beautiful to look upon, but she cannot be brought to regard whist as a serious science; as a partner of our joys and our woes, as a partner of everything else in life, she is immeasurably too good for us, but as a partner at whist she leaves much to be desired,—at whist one would gladly see her the partner of one's worst enemy, and then make the stakes as high as possible.

It is not thus that all ladies play. It was not thus that Sarah Battle played. And who was Sarah Battle? Charles Lamb shall answer that question in his own words: "'A clear fire, a clean hearth, and the rigor of the game.' This was the celebrated wish of old Sarah Battle, who, next to her devotions, loved a good game of whist,"—and who, it would appear, played an uncommonly good game, too. One can imagine the old lady sitting very upright indeed, with an eye as clear and flashing as her fire, with a mob-cap as white and spotless as her hearth, and with a rigor of deportment that was unequalled even by the rigorous laws of her favorite game. And one can imagine, also, Elia sitting opposite to her, with his respectful admiration a good deal tempered by the fearful timidity and awe inspired by his uncompromising partner. To only one weakness did she confess, and that only in the strictest confidence: she confessed that hearts was her favorite suit. This alone would serve to show how old-fashioned she was, and how long ago she must have lived. Nowadays, if any lady could be brought to confess to such a preference, it would be for diamonds. On the other hand, she did not approve of playing for love; she considered, and rightly, too, that some kind of stake was necessary to add a point and a zest to the game. Whist she declared to be the best of all games that she knew, because the partnership of two players divided the losses while it doubled the glory of winning. Probably old Sarah Battle, as well as Talleyrand, would have found a *triste vieillesse* without the solace of cards. But even while he admired the thoroughness and soundness of Sarah Battle's views, Elia could not refrain from putting in a plea for what he called "sick whist"; and we ourselves must confess to a sneaking liking for that humble game, although we may seem to have pointed at it with the finger of scorn. It was "sick whist" that the immortal Mr. Pickwick played at Dingley Dell with old Mrs. Wardle for his partner; but it was a very different whist that he played at Bath in company with Lady Snuphanuph, Mrs. Colonel Wugsby, and Miss Bolo, and probably he preferred the first to the rigor of the second game. On the latter occasion, if we remember rightly, his partner, Miss Bolo, "rose from the table considerably agitated, and went straight home in a flood of tears, and a sedan-chair." That is a failing shared by all ladies, even the best players; though they are generally careless of the stakes, they cannot bear to lose. But what would Miss Battle or Miss Bolo have said to the whist of New York? What would they have said!

The Spectator.

WHISTOLOGY.

"———the *Play*'s the thing
To touch the conscience of the king."

PROBABLY human ingenuity has not displayed itself in any discovery more than by the various modes it has invented to read the character, and detect the temperament, of individuals. This has been a favorite study from the very earliest ages—chiromancy existed among the Chaldeans, phrenology is of our own day—while sect after sect preferred their claim to attention, founding their several systems, now upon physical attribute, now upon some apparently adventitious element; so that, from the facial angle or the occipital ridge, to the shape of a man's nails, there is nothing which has not been admitted as evidence of his moral tendencies, or his intellectual capacity.

We have given years of patient thought and labor to this theme. We have revolved it long and arduously, discussing much with the learned of many lands, and our triumph it is at length to declare, that we believe success has crowned our life toil, and that we have arrived at the test of all temperament, the gauge of morals and the measure of mind. That we have, in short, established an ordeal which no subtlety can evade, no astuteness escape from; an ordeal, too, so comprehensive as to include the whole nation of men subjected to it, giving the measure of greatness and goodness, littleness or incapacity, as unerringly as the balance decides upon weight, and thus supplying to the world, bored with competitive trials and civil service commissions, one sure and safe measure by which it shall select its public men.

Among the many objections which will be started against his plan, there will be none more constantly put forward than its extreme simplicity—the old stumbling-block of weak minds, who require that truth not only should see at the bottom of the well, but that the water should be muddy besides. To such persons, however, he makes no appeal. To them he says: "Lovers of the inexplicably confused— ye men who worship complexity without consistency, and moderation without a purpose— go hence! *Your* teachers are members of Parliament! *Your* school-house is the British House of Commons, or a botanical lecture-room. The audience I seek is of those eager for truth, even though it come in the humblest garb, and with the smallest parade of pretension. To them, then, do I declare, that whist is the touchstone of humanity—the gauge and measure of man." "Whist!" exclaims some rash objector, "why, whist is a game—a mere game." Doubtless it is; but is not law a game? Is not medicine a game? Is not public life in its very highest walks a game? Is not literature a game—a mere game, with all its accidents of good and ill, its opportunities gained or lost, its poor hands occasionally played fortunately, and its trumps as often squandered? To suppose that by the word "game" deprecation must be understood, is to make a gross mistake. All the world is a vast play-table, with the heaviest stake that can be played for on the board. In the same way, but in a far more applicable sense, that the chase is said to be mimic war, a game may be the counterfeit of life, with all its vacillating changes, its failures and successes, its short-comings and its triumphs, its struggles and its accomplishments.

"I concede also this," cries another and more eager opponent; "but what becomes of your theory in the case of those—and a large majority of people they make—who do not play, never played, and probably never will play it?" To that I reply, that where a watch has no dial-plate I do not pretend to tell the hour. For the sake of that large and benighted class, I am ready with my sympathy and my sorrow. I regret heartfully that so much of intellectual culture has been denied them, even to the pitying expression of Prince Talleyrand to the unhappy man who confessed he had never learned the game: "Ah, my friend, what a wretched old age awaits you!" To tell me that the test is a fallacy, because it is not of universal application, is absurd; for what test is there that has such conditions? School experiences, for instance, make sad work of one's occipital ridge. I myself had four of them before I was on the "fifth form." Single-stick will do as much or more for your facial angle. A rowing-match against time will contribute generously to the characteristic indications of the palm of your hand; and as to the shape of your hat, if you wear a Gibus or a Jim Crow, you may defy all the "experts" of Europe.

I go no further, remember, than saying that whist is the test of those who play it; and I no more apply it to the outer barbarians who do not, than I would prescribe the ascent of Mont Blanc to a bishop. I am ready, as I told you above, to deplore tearfully that the number is not millions. I'd be pleased to think that even in our own colonies, scattered as they are over the universe, a rubber could always be found; and that while I write these lines—it is now nearing midnight—men were scoring the honors at Newfoundland, and marking the trick at Auckland.

Let no rash opponent burst in by saying : "Is it thus he speaks of a frivolous pastime? Does he want to dignify as a science a vulgar amusement, or establish as a test of capacity mere skill at a game?" Nothing of the kind, most hasty and intemperate of critics. With the amount of skill or ignorance a man may display at whist I have little concern. It is not of whist as a game I am treating, though I may add, in a parenthesis, that when I shall have addressed myself to the subject, Hoyle and Major A. will figure at a low mark in cheap catalogues, and even Deschapelles may be had for the "binding."

No ; my present business is with whist ethically considered—whist regarded as the emblem of the man whisting—and it is in the elimination of this as a theory that I lay claim to the honor of a discoverer. There may be some who will not accord me the patience, slight though it be, I crave ; some are already throwing down this paper ; some have arrived at the condemnatory "Pshaw, what folly!" But you, dear and valued reader, are not like these men—you will hear me for "my cause."

Let me, then, start with the declaration that whist includes a large range of high qualities, and a great extent of acquirement. The great whist-player must have patience, charity, forgiveness, forbearance, promptitude, considerable readiness in emergency, fortitude under calamity, a clear faculty to calculate probabilities, an admirable memory, and a spirit at once self-reliant and trustful. Not alone must he be graced by these bright endowments, but be bland in manner, and a courtier in demeanor, and be able to exercise every one of these qualities at the moment of requirement, showing himself at the self-same instant of time mature in thought, quiet in action—a Murat in pursuit, a Massena in resistance, and a D'Orsay in politeness! Whist, you are aware, is a perfect illustration of the law of evidence. You are given certain facts as the basis by which others are to be elicited. Your partner—I am speaking, of course, of one deserving of that name, one versed in the game, educated in its wisest precepts, himself a man of capacity, and animated by that spirit of responsibility which is the very essence of a player, and which whispers to him at each moment, "It is not my own fate that is alone at stake, there is a fellow-creature associated with me here; shall I by this knave bring joy to his heart, or will that club add another white hair to his whiskers?" Such a man as this, I say, gravely arranging his cards with a mingled caution and quickness, leads a card, as the French say, "invites." From that moment the issue of the cause opens: his card is the first witness on the table; that witness may be a person of mark or note, he may be one of the middle rank of life, or some humble creature, some deuce of diamonds, merely sent forward, like a picket, to fire a shot and fall back. Whatever be the card, the question of evidence is opened, and as speedily do you ask yourself: "What does this imply?" The resources of your own hand aid you in the answer, and you are in an instant in possession of the motive. Now it may be that, fully appreciating the intention, and rightfully estimating all your partner's resources, yet still the amount of support he expects from *you* is not available. Your object is, therefore, at once to show him that you cannot come up to his aid, that you are weak in that arm of the service, and that the order of attack must be altered.

You were a chief justice a moment back—you are a general in command now. The adversary has played, and what a flood of light breaks in upon you! You perceive immediately the indication of strength in a certain color, consequently, the likelihood of weakness in some other suit, since Fortune generally deals in these caprices; and thus thinking, your imagination soars upward on the speculation of that strength and that weakness. He has this, but not that; he wishes for a club; he is afraid of the diamonds. The fancy thus exercised attains an ease and pliancy you have not experienced before, and you see, almost without knowing it, a pack! Now comes the strong attack—or is it really strong? Is not that king led out so boldly a single card? and is this pretended strength not weakness, a mere bid of the opposition, which cannot deceive an old habitué of the Treasury benches? Ah, crafty politician that you are, how you have detected the clever bid for popular favor! but you are not to be the dupe of such an artifice. You are called on to reply; and now what a demand is suddenly made upon your memory, not alone for every card that has been played—that is a slight effort—but for every motive and impulse that suggested the play, and where the intention had met success, where failure; why your partner discontinued this or persisted in that; from what cause did he slight that advance, why seem to encourage that apparent failure. To your gifts of Lord Campbell, Napier, and Disraeli, you now add the calculating powers of a Babbage, all shrouded under the benevolence of a bishop, and the bland urbanity of a lord in waiting.

As I must not rob my other and *magnum opus* of details of this sort, you will excuse my pressing this theme any further. I merely mean, by these few and passing remarks, to call your attention to the true nature of the game, and the qualities it requires. If you see by this that the great player must of necessity be a man of varied and remarkable gifts, you will also perceive how, in the deficiency of such qualities, inferior performers exhibit manifold traits of this nature, the wants of the intellectual man being, so to say, eked out and supplied by the resources of the moral man. The great artist, perfect and complete, answering to every demand, ready at any emergency, is a grand and a very imposing spectacle. He stands out like some faultless statue that you walk around with ever-increasing admiration. Still, in the high exercise of his genius, his true nature is little revealed, for neither successes elate nor reverses surprise him, and *he* is not the profitable subject of contemplation.

It is your erring mortal, your whister, "not too good for human nature's daily food," your man of weaknesses and frailties, yielding to temptation here, trustful to rashness there; now credulous, now doubting; over-confident at one moment, over-cowardly the next; spendthrift to-day, miserly to-morrow; rash with his aces, and a niggard of some beggarly small trump, that might have spared his partner an "honor." This is the man for our purpose; watch him, mark him, even for one rubber, and you'll know more of his real innate actual nature than his wife knows, who has been solacing and scolding him for five-and-twenty years. Look at the very manual indecision with which he extricates that card from his hand, and seems, even as he plays, half to recall it. Mark how his eyes follow it—his own card—not the adversary's, nor his partner's, but his own blessed four of spades, and a worthless adventure, of no value to any one, but a whole argosy to him, for it was once *his*, and *he* played it. That man's heart is all selfishness. I know it. I see it. You may argue till you are blue, but you'll not persuade me to the contrary. Place him in a cabinet to-morrow, and he'll only have a thought for the measure he initiates himself—a measure probably of equal pretension with his four of spades. He is a one-idea'd creature, and the one idea is himself.

"Who led that card? How is all this? What's to play?" exclaims the sandy-eyebrowed man, with his long upper lip, and you see one who is always asking his way in life: begging this man to explain that leader in the Times, and beseeching every one to guide him somewhere. He is a bore, too, of that terrible category, the lackadaisical, making physical cold-bloodedness stand for breeding, and thinking himself the pink of fashion when supremely impertinent. Well, he'll meet his reward from that sharp-nosed old gentleman with the upstanding hair, and who has just turned the trick, as he would turn the key on a prisoner. Watch the unrelenting severity of that wicked old face as he leads out his trumps. Would n't he burn heretics! Would n't he thrash his nigger, think ye! No, he'll not leave you one—not one, sir; his memory has not begun to fail him yet, and he remembers you have the ten, though you have just played the knave. There is a savage sort of haste, too, in the way he gathers up the tricks—he is afraid your sufferings might have even a second's respite. And oh, poor benighted little man with the large cravat and the mosaic pin, what possessed you to keep all your good cards to be trumped, holding back your notes till the bank broke? You were a miser, that's the secret of it, and you thought to carry off your wealth with you at last. At all events, you could n't part with it. It was so pleasant to turn it over and look at it, and mutter, "Oh, I could make a show if I would; but I won't. I'll leave it to those silly fools there to squander their substance; but I'll die rich!"

We now come to the distrustful player, the man who has no faith in his partner, and who, forgetful that his efficiency is entirely dependent upon a thorough good understanding with his colleague, bores along alone and unseconded. This is a lamentable spectacle, and full of its moral teaching. You see such a man exactly as he would figure in the real world of life, ever encountering difficulties which only need the slightest amount of assistance to combat, but which, unaided, were insurmountable. You see him marring and deranging what might have proved skilful combinations but for his dogged and stubborn self-reliance. Next in order of hopelessness is the uncertain, wavering player; the man deterred by every chance obstacle, and continually altering his plans to suit some supposed necessity. He flies from hearts to spades, and from spades to diamonds; and if you watch him in the actual world, you will see such a man desert his party in the House, or his friends out of it, whenever an adverse incident seems to threaten them with misfortune.

Look at that careless fellow with the merry eye and the laughing mouth, and tell me, as he plays out all his best cards one after the other, if you do not recognize the spendthrift, that only lives on the present, and takes no heed for the future? One half of that abundance he is dissipating would have achieved a victory if only expended with judgment and discretion; but he does n't care for that; does n't care when his melancholy partner explains how and and why they have been beaten, but, with some wise saw about being jolly under difficulties, is quite ready to begin again, and be worsted, as he was before.

Is there a mood of man, is there an element of mind, or quality of temper, we have not here before us? The sanguine, the hopeless, the rash, the timid, the impetuous, the patient, the forgiving, the relentless, the easily baffled, and the stubbornly courageous man, are all there; and there is also the man of memory and the man of none. The man playing out his game—just as he lives—from hand to mouth; no calculation, no foresight, no care for the future in his heart; and there is, sad spectacle! the wretched creature who loses his game rather than play some paltry trump; and that man—take my word for it—would not spend sixpence in a cordial to restore life to the poor fellow rescued from drowning. Don't tell me this judgment of him is harsh, hasty or cruel. I have made these men my study. I have tracked them home at night, and seen them walk drearily back to their lodgings in the rain, rather than bestow a shilling for a cab, though the rheumatism and the cough will turn out to be a costlier luxury afterwards.

Another variety also deserves mention, and it

is one with which every whister must be familiar. The man who cares nothing about the game and everything for the stake; the man who has no interest in the changeful fortunes of the fight, but is intently interested in the result, and everlastingly inquiring, "What was the amount of the rubber?" as if the arithmetic was the real subject for anxiety. Such are, I grieve to own, the class who form successful men in the world. They look only to "what pays," and in this one-idea'd pursuit of the profitable, they always beat out of the field those poor souls who have notions of credit, character, and distinction.

As for that sanguine but not strong-headed individual who never suspects the adversary's strength, in the suit he has just led, because it has been suffered to go round once unmolested, I see the germs of an unfortunate speculator, the victim of Spanish "Threes"—"Poyais preference shares."

But as "there are manners of men," so are there whist-players, and it would only be to catalogue the moods of the one to enumerate the types of the other: The blindly hopeful creature, that will play his game out without the faintest shadow of a chance in his favor, true emblem of the fellow who actually does not know he is ruined till he reads his name as bankrupt in the Gazette; and his antitype, the melancholy, despondent man, who, with four by honors, expects defeat, portraying the rich annuitant, who awakes every morning with the horror that he is to end his days in a poor-house. And let us not forget the plodding, hesitating, long-meditating player, who will not lay down on the table some miserable deuce of clubs without five minutes of what he fancies to be consideration. Go not to that man with a subscription-list for a poor family, ask not him to join you in a little effort to buy winter clothing for the naked, or firing for the shivering and destitute; he will listen to you for an hour, if you like, but he will never give you a farthing.

I have taken all the dark sides of the medal here, as my readers will perceive. I have recorded none of those grand, heroic, self-devoting traits with which whist abounds; I have said nothing about those noble bursts of confidence with which this man will sacrifice his all that his partner may be triumphant; as little mention have I made of those beautiful little episodes of charity, those touching instances of tender pity with which your great player overlooks the irregularities of some weak and erring adversary. Wonderfully affecting incidents, too, when one remembers that they come out in the very ardor of conflict: it is giving quarter in the thick of the battle, and amidst the dead and the dying. In fact, I am only fearful that if I but venture out farther on the vast ocean of Illustration, I may never see land again. Perhaps, however, I have set the stone in motion, and other stronger hands will now lend it the impulse of a push. Perhaps the great moralist of the age, whoever he be, will revolve this theory in his mind, and render its application popular and easy. Perhaps who knows but the wise men they call Civil Service Commissioners may introduce whist into the list of subjects for examination, and tide-waiters be questioned on the " odd trick "?

At all events, I trust that I have shown that whist has its ethical phase: that no man playing it can, no matter what his proficiency or his ignorance, no matter how eager or indifferent he may be, no matter how subtle to subdue emotion, or how guarded to cloak his wishes,— no man, I repeat, can shroud his real nature in obscurity, but must stand out revealed, and declared in his true character. The test is one that no subterfuge can escape from, no ingenuity evade.

"*Le style c'est l'homme*," was the old maxim of a once famed philosopher, but a wiser age repudiates the adage, and proclaims that it is "whist is the man." With this declaration I have done. "*Exegi monumentum*"; to others I bequeath all the benefit of my researches, all the profit of my labors. The rubber is over. Good night!

All The Year Round.

WHIST AT OUR CLUB.

A T our club, which is a most respectable club, a good deal of whist has been played during the last ten or twenty years. The time was when men used to meet together o' nights for the sake of cards and gambling. It was thus that Fox and his friends used to—I was going to say amuse themselves, but I fear that with them the diversion went beyond amusement. But with us at our club there is nothing of that kind. There are perhaps a dozen gentlemen, mostly well stricken in years, who, having not much else to do with their afternoons, meet together and kill the hours between lunch and dinner. I do not know that they could find a wiser expedient for relieving the tedium of their latter years. I have said that they have nothing to do with their afternoons. I doubt whether many of them have much to do with their mornings. Breakfast, the newspaper, perhaps a letter or two, with a little reading, carry them on to lunch and their glass of sherry. After that there may be a little walking, or perhaps some gentle exercise on an easy cob, a slight flutter of impatience, and then at length the hour of delight has come. Between three and four the party is assembled, and the delight is reached which, for us, makes easy the passage to the grave.

Every one knows how Talleyrand, the reputed father of all modern French good sayings is supposed to have remarked that he who did not learn to play cards was preparing for himself a melancholy old age. In looking round at these bald, gray, wrinkled, and somewhat infirm companions of mine, who are gentlemen, and have, some of them, done something in the world, I am often disposed to declare to myself that whoever said that saying spoke the truth. If we were not playing whist, what should we be doing?

There comes a time of life when the work of life naturally ceases. The judge becomes deaf and resigns. The active civil servant is active no longer, and either takes a pension, or escapes early from his desk. The lawyer has made his fortune, or is forced to give way to newer men. The capacity for twelve hours of labor is at any rate gone. Books cannot be read for ever. If the mind would stand it—which it will not—the eyes would fail. Cricket, rowing, deer-stalking, even hunting and shooting are all gone. The women will not let you make love to them—unless you are rich and a bachelor, and then the love-making is soon over. What else should an old gentleman do? If he can say his prayers all the time, or give himself up to continued meditation and the "labelling of his thoughts"—if he can dream Platonic Utopias, or theorize in his arm-chair on that still undiscovered "greatest good"— then he may sink down quietly without the assistance of a card-table. To some, but only to a few, can it be given to relieve the tedium of a *fainéaut* existence by the consciousness of the dignity of a parliamentary bench. If you can become a legislator, you may get through your hours, uneasily indeed, but with the satisfaction of self-importance. But if none of these things suffice for you or be open to you, it will be well for you when you are old that you shall know something of the rules of whist and belong to such a club as ours.

I do not think that there is among us much propensity to gambling. Some have, indeed, a keen eye to their money; but they look rather to holding themselves harmless, and having their amusement for nothing, than to the making of any profit. One or two are perhaps buoyed up with the hope that the day may come when they shall make something, though the day never seems to come. Some are manifestly indifferent, taking and paying their shillings without a feeling. I do not think that these get so much amusement out of the proceeding as it ought to give. We have one old gentlemen who evidently likes to pay. The glory of making a trick is all the world to him; but though he has played cards for many years, he never seems quite to have reconciled himself to the idea of taking money out of another man's pocket.

We play shilling points. Any member of the club who comes into that room can join any table which is not yet full at shilling points. And, as a rule, this modest limit is preserved. If, now and again, two gentlemen choose to bet a sovereign, no complaint is made. The habit is distasteful to the majority; but a club is a club, and men like to feel themselves free. As long as the rules of the club are not broken, the co-partners at the table cannot complain. In this way occasionally a little excitement is added; but I do not think that the life, the spirit, the noise, the evident vivacity, and the generally happy disposition of the room, depend upon the gambling. If it did, there would be no content; for I know no one who wins, and no one who loses. In spite of these sovereign bets, which perhaps are becoming a little more frequent than they used to be, I do not think that in our club anybody is ever injured in the way of money. They can afford to pay the stakes they lose, and are none the better for what they win. It is not thence that the excitement comes, and yet there is a great deal of excitement.

Excitement is a great step towards happiness, particularly to those who are over sixty. Cicero has put into the mouth of the orator Antony an opinion which certainly was not his own. He makes Antony say that leisure—the doing of nothing—is the sweetest resource of old age. Old men have often said so ; but foxes also have often said that grapes were sour. Old men are as fond of activity, as much given to excitement, as prone to keep themselves busy, and to have what we may call a full life, as their juniors ; but these delights do not come easily to them.

The failure in our powers, which envious nature prepares for us, affects our body, and perhaps unfortunately our minds, before it touches our wills. The lean and slippered pantaloon would be as full of wise instances as the justice, if he could get any one to hear him ; and the justice would, but for shame, be as full of strange oaths, and as jealous in honor, if not as quick in quarrel, as the soldier. The old man likes excitement if he can find it; and they who frequent the next room to the whist-room at our club say that we have been successful in our search. Voices could not be so loud, contradictions so frequent, rebukes so rife—there could not be such rising storms, nor then such silent lulls, unless the occupation in hand were one on which those occupied were very much intent. The silence is as notable as the voices—and they are very notable; a dozen men could not be so suddenly and so awfully silent unless engaged on something which fills their very souls with solicitude. And certainly no dozen men could make such a row—gentlemen too, old gentlemen, respectable old gentlemen—unless they were very much in earnest.

I think the charm in our club comes from the fact that no one plays very well, but that we know enough of the rules to talk about them and to think that we play in accordance with them. All the recognized treatises on the game are in the room. We have taken great care on that point; and our allusions to Clay, Cavendish, and the great professors are so frequent as to make an unaccustomed bystander suppose that not one of us is ignorant of any one enunciated law. But the knowledge of laws and the practice of them are different things, especially when the practice has to be instantaneous, and when its efficacy depends on the memory of all that has gone before. Now I find that at our club everybody remembers his own cards, or, at any rate, those on which he has based his hopes of success, while no one remembers his partner's cards. But that the latter is the special memory which his partner expects from him. Therefore, there is often a diversity of opinion.

I take it for granted that the injustice of each is never apparent to himself—the injustice of always demanding from another exactly that trouble which the unjust player never takes himself. "Good ———! I played you the eight of spades, and you trumped it with the last trump, though you must have known that the seven was the only one left!" Then the enraged speaker tears his hair and looks around. Or perhaps he is of a saturnine nature—more severe, but less demonstrative. "Well, Dr. Pintale, if you call that whist, I don't." Upon that the severe one purses his lips together and is silent, intending to impress upon the company around a conviction that Dr. Pintale's capacity for whist is of such a nature that words would be altogether thrown away upon him. Dr. Pintale for the moment is cowed. There is not a word to be said in excuse. No doubt he has thrown away a trick which a good player would have saved. He knows in his own heart that his dear friend, Sir Nicholas Bobtail, the partner who has just so severely punished him, and who, in any other matter, would move heaven and earth to succor him, never remembers the sevens and eights himself. Sir Nicholas makes as many blunders as anybody in the club, but has a sharp way of snarling, which often saves him from the criticism of his friends. Poor Dr. Pintale is meekness itself, till roused by exaggerated injuries, when sometimes he will say a word. "I do call that rather hard," continues Sir Nicholas, turning to one of his adversaries. "With that trick we should just have been out, and I have n't won a rubber this afternoon." Poor Pintale sits quiet and repentant, but patting his soft fat hands together under the table as the irritation rises to his gentle heart. "I wish you 'd tell me why you did it, Dr. Pintale?" asks Sir Nicholas, as though he really wanted information on the matter.

Pintale would not have minded it so much had he not been called "Doctor." The Doctor and Sir Nicholas have been friends for the last thirty years. For all these years they have been "Bobtail" and "Pintale" to each other, long before any decorative letters, any D. C. L. or K. C. B. had been appended to their names. Either would have been prepared to write an epitaph for the other, attributing to him all the virtues which can adorn a man, a friend, and a Christian. But when you have petted up your penultimate best card, and have succeeded in extracting all the trumps except that happy remnant in your partner's hand; when all your manœuvres have been successful, and fortune has sat square upon your brow; when the delightful moment has come for showing to friends and foes how complete has been your strategy,—then to be crushed by the fatuous inattention of your own ally—that is too much for human friendship! It is as though one's own wife should turn against one in one's own profession.

"I wonder why he did do it?" said Sir Nicholas, turning round to one of the expectant bystanders.

"I've seen you make the same mistake yourself fifty times," says the Doctor, pressed beyond his bearing.

"That's a mere *tu quoque*," says the K. C. B.

"I've seen you do it a hundred times—two hundred times," rejoins the D. C. L., very red in the face. Then the door is opened, and somebody looks in from the passages; after which the matter is allowed to drop, the Doctor having evidently become a little ashamed of himself.

The wonderful thing in whist is this,—that ignorance of any of those intricate rules by which the game is governed is regarded as so disgraceful that nobody will admit it ; nor will any one allow that he is wanting in that perfect and prolonged practice without which no proficient in any art can bring his rules to bear at the moment in which they are wanted ; and yet players generally would be ashamed to have it supposed that they had devoted to a mere game of cards so great a proportion of their intellect and their time as to have mastered these rules, and to have familiarized themselves with the practice. Who would not be ashamed to be known as a first-class billiard-player, and to confess an intimacy so close with pockets, chalk, and ivory balls as to have left himself time for no more worthy pursuit? For to play billiards as billiards can be played requires the energy of a life. Nor even will an ambitious man, or one who desires success in a profession, be anxious to be accounted among the grand chess-players of the day. The art of chess-playing, excellent as it is, does not lead to results great enough in themselves to justify the expenditure of labor and intelligence which is necessary for perfection. We may say the same of all those amusements which have by means of their own success so run over their original boundaries as to have become the subject of scientific study. Here and there a man has the leisure and the intellect, and in the absence of a higher ambition he devotes his life to elucidate a game. We admire his ingenuity, but we do not think very much of his career. There is something better to be done in the life of all of us than chess, or billiards, or whist. In regard to the two former, no one demands that others shall play well. But in whist it seems to be implied that if a man does not know and practise all the rules which have ever been invented, he ought to be ashamed of himself! This is carried so far in our club that every player is presumed to know all the rules—and to depart from them, not from inexperience, not from ignorance, not from temporary aberration of mind, but from some devilish malignity which has induced him at that moment to do evil that others might be tormented.

At our club the main rules are known. They

are so frequently discussed that it is impossible that we should forget them. Clay and Cavendish are in our hands at every turn. With five trumps, the worst amongst us would lead a trump. When we are weak ourselves, we do not force our partners. We know how to *finesse* a queen, and I think we generally count the trumps,—at any rate, early in the afternoon. There are laws the keeping of which does not require the player to travel much beyond the consideration of his own cards. But we have not arrived at the reading of our partner's hands, and hence chiefly come those angry words and fiery looks, which do upon the whole, I think, increase rather than diminish our enjoyment. If I throw away a card from a weak suit, it is certainly a grievous thing to have a low card in that very suit at once led me, and to know that this has been done because my partner would not take the trouble to watch the card as it fell from my hand. The stormiest five minutes that I ever remember came from such a cause as this. Our Mr. Polden—everybody knows old Dick Polden as one of the softest-hearted human beings that ever became the prey to begging letter-writers and weeping women—does not play very well himself. He is an eager, excitable man, whose mind never remains fixed long on the same thing, and who, I may say, almost invariably forgets to practise the care which he expects others to exercise in his behalf. I do not think that he is really choleric, but he has an unfortunate tone of voice and a trick of eyebrow which make a bystander think sometimes that he will very soon proceed to blows. Those who know him are aware that he is not himself conscious at these moments of exceeding the mildest forms of friendly remonstrance. He was playing not long since with Admiral Green as his partner. The Admiral is a very constant attendant at our club, and perhaps the best player that we have. He is generally a quiet man, but he has a nasty habit of looking round and smiling when his partner makes an egregious blunder, which some of us dislike worse even than being objurgated. On this occasion, Dick Polden had two strong suits in his hand, and one was weak; but on the whole he was playing what he considered a great game. He had called for trumps, and had thrown away a card from his weak suit. We who were playing against him, I and poor, dear Grimley—Sir Peter Grimley, who has since been taken away from us—knew well what Polden was about. At such moments he wriggles in his chair, raises his body a couple of inches in triumphant expectation, and tells the whole tale of his heart to those who watch him.

How it was that such a player as the Admiral should at such a moment have led from the discarded suit, none of us could understand.

Grimley declared that it was intended as a rebuke to poor Polden's somewhat noisy anticipation. I never could believe that, as the Admiral is fond of his money, which on this occasion he not only risked, but lost. As soon as the peccant card showed itself on the table, Polden lost all control. "Good ———!" he exclaimed, raising both his hands, quite indifferent to the fact that he was thus showing all his cards. "Polden," said the baronet, "that is not whist." "No," said Polden, very hotly;

"No; certainly it is not whist. Of course he saw my heart; he could n't but see it. Everybody knows that he sees everything. I wonder, Grimley, what you would have said if that had happened to you?"

"I should have sworn horribly; but it would have been inwardly, so that no one would have heard me," said Grimley.

"And what would he have said if I had done it to him?" continued Polden. Perhaps of all forms of abuse, that of addressing yourself to a third person, and of calling your sinning partner "he" or "him," is the most provoking. During all this time the game was going on, and the Admiral had only smiled. At every new contortion of Polden's face the Admiral smiled again; and as Polden became all contortions, so did the Admiral become all smiles. At last the climax was reached. A queen from Polden's long suit of spades was taken by the king, and then his ace was trumped. All this misfortune, no doubt, had come from the Admiral's blunder. Polden's case was one of great hardship, but when he flung down his cards, declaring that he could n't play against three adversaries, and when his cards were therefore called, and when the Admiral quietly showed that had they been kept up the game might have been saved,—then it was evident, even to Polden himself, that he had been in the wrong. And he was a man who could dare anything while hot passion gave him the consciousness of right, but who was cowed at once when a feeling that he was in fault had crept in upon him. When the proof had been made perfect that the game might have been saved, he passed his hand over his bald head, and sank back, tamed, upon his chair.

"No doubt," said the Admiral, taking the two packs of cards under his two hands, so as to prevent the immediate continuation of the play; "no doubt I made a mistake with that heart."

"Let us say no more about it," said Polden.

"A few words, if you please. We will wait half a minute, if you do not object, Sir Peter." For Grimley, knowing what was coming, had made an attempt to get at one of the packs, so as to lessen, by action, the strength of the

Admiral's coming attack. "I made a foolish mistake. But I do not think that that justified you in throwing your arms about like a demented windmill. I was driven by your words and actions and looks to think whether in kindness we ought not to speak to your friends." Had the Admiral spoken in an angry tone there would have been nothing in it. We are so used to angry tones, and have become so conscious that they are to be regarded as merely an organ accompaniment to our generally pleasant music, that had the Admiral condescended to be noisy, we should simply have been anxious to get hold of the cards and begin again. But his tranquillity afflicted us all, and absolutely quelled poor old Polden.

"You're making too much of it," said the Baronet.

"Not at all," said the Admiral. "I shall expect Mr. Polden to apologize."

Apologize! that was more than any of us could stand. A crowd of men from the other tables had now congregated round us. Among us all Dick Polden was, perhaps, the most generally popular. Who but he would give up his right to a place to another player? Who but he would remain beyond his time to make up a rubber for others? Who but he would take the chair close to the fire if it were hot, or expose his shoulder to the window if it were cold? When did Polden willingly tread on any man's corn, or fail to soothe any man's vanity? When little subscriptions have had to be raised, who has ever known Polden to refuse his guinea? It was out of the question that he should be reduced to the ignominy of an apology. And, moreover, the very fact of an apology having been demanded and given would be evidence of a quarrel, and it had always been a point with us to declare that, though we were loud, we never quarrelled. We should have been ashamed of our excitability as respectable old gentlemen had we not always been able to assert that each loud enunciation had been simply an amusing incident of our game. When the Admiral spoke of an apology, we all felt that he was ignorant of the very nature of the bond which united us. If we could not bear each other's ways without apologies, the whist must be given up. And from dear old Polden too, who at this moment was almost in tears!

"I don't think that can be necessary," said Dr. Absolom. Dr. Absolom had once been one of the royal doctors, and is a man of authority. By dint of a commanding brow and a loud, steady voice he has acquired a sort of influence over us. His whist is not good, but no one ventures to scold him much. "Perhaps, doctor, if you had played so and so," is the extent to which we go with him. "If I had, the event might perhaps have been different," he will reply with dignity. The altercation with Dr. Absolom is never carried beyond that.

"Perhaps, Dr. Absolom, you did not hear the remarks which were made," said the angry Admiral.

If I love any one, I love Polden.

"I heard them," said I, "and they were very fierce. But I should have thought that we all understood Polden's ferocity by this time."

"Was I fierce?" asked Polden piteously.

"I should think you were," said the Baronet,

"and so should I have been. But as for apologies, bless my soul! if we come to that we had better give it all up." Then there was a general acclamation that nothing more was to be said about it, during which the Admiral subsided. For the next day or two he was rather stiff in his manner to Mr. Polden, but before the end of the week everything was right again.

That, I think, was the nearest approach to a quarrel that we ever had, and a rumor of it I fear, got through the club. But in answer to all questions we have all of us been firm in our assertions that there was no quarrel.

That system of "calling" is, of all self-imposed torments, the most tormenting. Readers, no doubt, will understand what "calling" means. When you wish your partner to lead you a trump, you play your cards from some other suit out of their proper course—throwing down, say, the ten on the first round, and the deuce on the second. Players, I think, are generally of opinion that it injures the game—and no doubt it does more harm than good if the partner who is called to does not see the call.

But it has this advantage, that it gives an indifferent player a great facility for playing a game of his own, and for scolding his partner for not assisting him. It creates an equality. For though it may be difficult to observe a call, nothing can be easier than calling itself. "You did n't see my call," says the injured one afterwards — or very frequently not waiting till afterwards.

"Did you call?"

"Well, rather. It would have made two tricks' difference—that's all."

Then the offending one, knowing that this must be an exaggeration, goes to work—not to defend himself, but to prove that at the outside one trick only would have been saved, had he been attentive.

It seems to me that at our club one's partner never sees a call, but that it is very often seen by the adversaries. Therefore, at our club, if you are particularly anxious that trumps should not be led, so that you may ruff this suit or the other, then is the time to call.

You have two adversaries, but only one partner. If you know your man, you may perhaps be almost sure that he will be blind;—and in this way you stop your enemy from playing his game, and get him to play yours.

"You have no right to look like that when you call," Sir Nicholas said the other day to Dr. Pintale.

"I may look as I please," said the Doctor.

"Certainly not. When you put down your second card in that way, and then look up at your partner, you might just as well say out loud what you want. I appeal to the table."

Dr. Absolom and Mr. Poser were playing. Mr. Poser is a young man under fifty, who has come in among us I hardly know why, and who writes poetry, which I hope is better than his whist. He is an amusing man, and we rather like having a poet.

"My friend, Dr. Pintale, is perhaps a little demonstrative," said Dr. Absolom.

"Lesbia hath a calling eye," sang Mr. Poser; "and some of us know for what he calleth."

Then it was presumed that the evidence had been adverse to Dr. Pintale; and he was constrained to promise that he would henceforth keep his features in better order.

Mr. Thompson's objection to the practice—a practice which he never could bring himself in the least to understand—was, I think, both true and picturesque. Mr. Thompson is a clergyman who, in former days, did the light work of a city parish, whose church has been pulled down, and who therefore, feeling that his own clerical position has been, as it were, stolen from him, disports himself, very quietly, like a layman. It is he who is so greedy of making tricks, and is so unwilling to take the money that he wins. He is an old man, of a sweet temperament, and much tinged with romance. "Why graft another thorn upon the rose?" said he—"and a sharper thorn than those with which nature has surrounded her?"

But in very truth it is the presence of the thorns which constitutes the delight of our whist. I used to think, when I would walk home from our club after a bout of scolding which had lasted the whole afternoon, that there was something in our eager words derogatory to the dignity of old age, and I have asked myself more than once whether it would not become me to abandon a pursuit which evidently could not be followed without hard words.

For I was soon convinced that whist without scolding was altogether out of the question. But after a little I began to think that the exercitation was in itself healthy. As a lot of boys on a playground together can hardly make too much noise as long as they do not fight, so in regard to old men, if they do not quarrel, why should they be restrained from that manifestation of interest which eager loud words evince? To sit and play whist dumb, or with casual word about the fire, or the table, or the state of the atmosphere, would be so dull that men could only be kept at it by some desire of making money. Of that stain there is, I think, nothing at our club. And therefore, when I found how strong was the determination to silence the Admiral when he talked about an apology—how resolute we all were that there should be no

acknowledgment of the evidence of a quarrel—
I reconciled myself to the noise, and took
comfort in assuring myself that whist, as played
at our club, is a wise resource for old gentlemen.

Blackwood's Magazine.

A HAND AT CARDS.*

CAVENDISH in his *Card Essays* gives us the story of "The Duffer Maxims," and some anecdotical matter of an amusing nature about the *talkers*. By way of appendix to sober instruction, we have thought to introduce the conversation *verbatim* during a single hand of four persons seated for the purpose of "playing whist," as each of them called the performance, —literally, however, a rollicking exhibition that should be named

PLAYING AT PLAYING WHIST.

The play is by the five-point game. The score is 0. C. deals and turns the 9 of hearts.

* By permission of the author and of Messrs. Houghton, Mifflin, & Co.

"There," says C., "That's the way you treat *me*. I never get an honor in the world, but when *I* cut, somehow, I always cut for somebody else."

B. takes up his hand, sorts it. It is composed of ace and 2 of spades, kn., 6, and 3 of hearts, qu., kn., 9, and 7 of diamonds, and 7, 6, 5, and 4 of clubs, and he begins the usual growl: "I should like to know how anybody is going to get anything out of this. I never *can* get a hand." [That is to say, he does not hold ace, k., and qu. of three plain suits, and the four honors in trumps. Give him these cards every time and he would be pleased to play whist.] "I suppose I must play something. There's a diamond; that's according to rule, anyhow," and throws the 7.

"You don't strike me very heavily," says D., "but I can follow suit," and throws the 6. He holds the k., 10, 8, 7, 6 of spades, the kn. and 7 of hearts, the ace, k., qu., and 2 of clubs, and the k. and 6 of diamonds.

"I can take that," says A., throwing the ace, "that is, unless it's trumped." He holds the

5, 4, and 3 of spades, the ace, qu., 10, 4 and 2 of hearts, the ace, 10, 8, 3, and 2 of diamonds, and no club. "Are you going to trump that, C.?"

"No," says C., "I can't trump anything, nor take anything either, I guess," and plays the 4. He holds the qu., kn., and 9 of spades, the 9, 8, and 5 of hearts, the kn., 10, 9, 8, and 3 of clubs, and the 5 and 4 of diamonds.

"Now," says A., "let's try a little trump," and throws the 4 of hearts.

"Coming at us early, are you?" says C., and he plays the 5.

"I'll try to get that," says B., and throws the kn.

"No you don't," says D., and bangs the k. upon the trick.

"Well, I did n't expect it," says B., "It was the best that I had. If we get out of this without losing the whole thing *I* shall be glad."

"Now," says D., "there's a club for you," throwing the k.

A. determines, "I'll let that travel," and throws the 3 of spades ; C. 3 of clubs, B. 4. "I did n't know but you might have the ace," said

A. to B. "He might have led from king and queen."

"Yes, that's so," said B.; "of course you could n't tell." [N. B. Trumping the trick would have made no difference in result.]

"Well, I'll have one of your trumps, anyway," says D., and throws the queen of clubs. A. trumps unwillingly with the 2 of hearts; C. plays the 8 of clubs, and B. the 5.

"Now, we'll see about this," says A., and plays the 10 of hearts. He remembers that the k. and kn. have fallen, and thinks he knows whist pretty well to lead the 10 now instead of the ace. C. plays 8, B. 3, and D. 7. "You have another," says A. to C., for he remembered the 9 was turned—another positive proof to himself of great proficiency in whist. A. qu., C. 9, B. 6, D. 6 of spades.

"Now I'll give my partner his suit." Proof number three of skill and information about the game; and he throws the 3 of diamonds, C. 5, B. kn., D. k.

"I'll have that trump anyhow," says D., and plays the ace of clubs, displaying *his* embracing knowledge of whist, that will not only not let a trump remain in the opponent's hand, but dares to sacrifice a high card to bring it out. D. ace of clubs, A. ace of hearts, C. 6 of clubs, B. 5 of clubs. Then A. plays 2 of diamonds, C. 9 of clubs, B. qu. of diamonds, D. 2 of clubs; B. 9 of diamonds, D. 7 of spades, A. 10 of diamonds, C. 10 of clubs; A. 8 of diamonds, C. 8 of spades, B. 7 of clubs, D. 9 of spades. Three rounds in silence. No help for it.

"Now," says D., "we 'll have something else." A. leads the 5 of spades, C. plays qu., B. ace, and D. 10.

"Any more aces?" says D.

"No, only a little spade that I suppose you will get," says B., and plays the 2, taken by D.'s king.

"All right, we 're three by card," says B. "I should never have guessed it by the looks of *my* hand."

"You must remember I helped you a little," says A.

"We stopped you from going out, that 's all that I thought we *could* do," says C.

"Well, we got all that there was; there did n't any of them get away," says A.

"Come on, it's my deal," says B., "cut the cards."

"Yes, and I suppose cut you an honor," says C.

And so the game goes charmingly on.

This and like to this, is the talk or the thought of hundreds of card-handlers. These players had no idea of what the cards they held were capable, and thought they were really playing them in accordance with their value.

Let us place the same cards in the hands of good American whist-players, who read them as they fall, drawing the inferences they offer, but under the law of their game speaking not a word, and I see how A. and B., *from the same beginning*, compel the entire game before the adversaries secure a trick.

B. throws the 7 of diamonds, the correct lead, from his hand; D. plays the 6. A. instantly reasons this wise: "My partner must have three higher cards. He cannot have k. and qu., or he would have led the k.; he cannot have k. and kn., or he would have lead the 9; he holds the qu., kn., and 9. The 6 is played on my right. D. is probably not calling, for I have five trumps. Either the k. is there alone, or D. has no more. If he has no more, k. with another held by C. will take at any rate. I must pass the trick to catch the card upon my right."

All this that takes so long to write and to read flashes instantaneously through the mind of a good player.

A throws the 3 of diamonds, for not only must he not play the ace, but he must not take the trick because he must not have the lead; C. throws the 4. B. at once takes in the situation and leads the highest of his trumps. D. can gain nothing by refusing to throw k. If A. has ace, and k. is not played, it will not cover kn.; and if C. has neither ace nor qu. (for B. can have neither of these), C. is to be helped by D.'s play, calling, in trumps, two honors for one. If A. holds both ace and qu., of course D.'s play is fruitless. B. kn. of hearts,

D. k., A. ace, C. 5.   A. draws the other trumps with qu. and 10, plays the ace of diamonds on which the k. must fall, and continues the diamonds,—B. having thrown the kn. on ace that he may be out of A.'s way, for from C.'s play of the 4 and 5 the rest of the diamonds are marked with A. B. having taken the small diamond next led with the qu., throws the ace of spades, as he sees that with A.'s diamonds and trumps the game is won. B. leads the 9 of diamonds, A. takes with the 10, plays the 8, and then the trumps; claiming five points and game.

As we close this text-book devoted to the students of the wondrous game, we kindly recommend those who are careless about the proprieties, to contrast the *manner* of this play of the same cards, to consider the folly of making remarks while the game is in progress, and to derive such satisfaction as they may from the illustration, that defines the difference between PLAYING WHIST and playing at playing whist.

American Whist Illustrated by G. W. P.

A WHIST PARTY.*

MR. GALANT (*who is an authority at his club*).—Are you fond of whist, Mrs. Bland?

MRS. BLAND (*his hostess and partner*).—Oh, immensely! I fear, though, I am a little out of practice.

MR. GALANT (*who has his misgivings about ladies' whist*).—Perhaps you would prefer a game of euchre?

MRS. BLAND.—Oh, no, indeed! I know how devoted you are to whist. Mr. Bland often speaks of your prowess.

MISS FICHU (*one antagonist*).—Oh, we *must* play whist. I shall be *too* proud if we win; and if we lose, it is only what we ought to expect.

* By permission of Messrs. Chas. Scribner's Sons.

YOUNG DARBY (*another antagonist*).—Why, you know, Mr. Galant, it is really awfully plucky our standing up against you at all!

MR. GALANT (*who does n't see much sport ahead for himself*).—Well, then, we 'll get to work. Will you ladies cut for the deal?

MRS. BLAND (*cutting an ace*).—Oh, dear, low deals, and I 've the very highest card in the pack!

MR. GALANT.—The deal is yours; ace is low in the deal cut

MRS. BLAND.—Oh, yes, I remember now. How stupid of me!

MR. GALANT (*involuntarily*).—Don't mention it!

MRS. BLAND (*looking at her cards*).—Fancy my dealing such a hand to myself! Mr. Galant, I hope I 've treated you better.

MR. GALANT (*dryly*).—Thanks.

MISS FICHU.—Have I got to lead? I do so hate to do that.

YOUNG DARBY (*encouragingly*).—If you 'll lead any one of three suits I 'll agree to take it.

MRS. BLAND.—But beware how you lead the fourth, for that I shall win.

MR. GALANT (*muses to himself*).—Three aces on my left and one in my partner's hand. This *is* whist.

MRS. BLAND (*later in the same hand*).—Well, there's the queen, too. I like to use up a suit while its fresh.

MISS FICHU.—So do I; it's so easy to remember about it then.

YOUNG DARBY (*trumping the trick*).—Your queen is doomed, though, Mrs. Bland.

MRS. BLAND.—Oh, Mr. Darby, that is n't polite at all. Now, that I think of it, you played the knave on my king, did n't you?

MR. GALANT (*faintly*).—Yes, ma'am.

MRS. BLAND.—Oh, how stupid of me! I might have known.

MR. GALANT (*at the end of the hand*).—You had good trump cards, Mrs. Bland. I presume you did not notice my trump signal?

MRS. BLAND.—Oh, I had forgotten all about that. I must watch next time!

Miss Fichu.—Oh, is it my lead again? Let me see—"When in doubt lead trumps."

Young Darby (*approvingly*).—A very good play, Miss Fichu.

Mrs. Bland.—But the trick is ours with my ace. Now, (*fingering a card,*) you led me something, Mr. Galant. What in the world was it?

Mr. Galant (*whose misgivings have become certainties*).—I can hardly tell you that, you know.

Mrs. Bland.—Of course not. How unfortunate that I do not recall it, though; it was a heart or a diamond.

Miss Fichu (*facetiously*).—Lead both.

Mrs. Bland.—I wish I might. I'll follow your example, and solve my doubt in trumps.

Young Darby.—How charming of you, Mrs. Bland; I was so hoping you might.

Mrs. Bland.—Oh, Mr. Darby, did you want it?

Mr. Darby.—Above all things. Did n't you hear me applaud Miss Fichu's trump lead?

Mrs. Bland.—Of course you did. How very stupid!

Mr. Darby (*complacently leading his cards with a jerk*).—I believe the trumps are all out, and all my spades are good. Can you take this—or this—or this—oh, I miscounted. Mr. Galant has the last spade.

Mrs. Bland (*eagerly*).—Oh, what does that do?

Mr. Galant (*dryly*).—It gives them four instead of five.

Mrs. Bland (*quite relieved*).—Oh, you have saved the day, Mr. Galant!

Miss Fichu.—And we have won the game, with two to spare.

Mrs. Bland.—Oh, is that really so?

* * *

Miss Fichu (*on Young Darby's arm later, promenading the rooms*).—We have been playing whist with Mr. Galant. Do ask us who won four games out of five; we're too modest to proffer the information.

* * *

A Whist Party

MISS PARACHUTE (*to waiting friends*).—Oh, dear, I felt sure Mr. Galant could make a fourth hand at our game of whist, and I just begged him to do so; but he says he does n't know one card from another!

PHILIP H. WELCH.

AT BOVOR.—PLAY A GREAT GAME OF WHIST.*

EVENING after dinner. On the moat in a punt with Englefield. Dark night: cold: damp: romantic but for this. Englefield says, abruptly, "Capital point." I ask here, what? He replies, "Two fellows, one the Villain, the other Injured Innocence, in punt: real water easily done on the stage. Villain suddenly knocks Injured Innocence into the water: he sinks: is caught in the weeds below: never rises again. Or, on second thought, is n't drowned, but turns up somehow in the last Act." I own it a good idea, and propose going in-doors, as I see Mrs. Childers making tea.

* By permission of the author and of Messrs. Bradbury, Agnew, & Co., London, and of Messrs. Roberts Brothers, Boston.

In-doors.—Stenton, the philosopher, says, "Tea is an incentive. So much tea is found in every man's brain." Poss says it ought to be a caution to anybody not to use hot water to his face, or he might turn his head into a tea-pot. I'm sorry Poss turns this interesting theme into ridicule, as I like hearing Stenton's conversation. He has a deep bass voice which is very impressive. There is a pause. Considering that we are all more or less clever here, it is wonderful how dull we are. I suppose that the truth is we avoid merely frivolous and commonplace topics. Englefield, who is a nuisance sometimes, suddenly looks at me, and asks me "to say something funny." I'm glad they know nothing of the Pig-squeaking song.

I smile on him pityingly. Childers says, "Come, you're last from town, haven't you got any good stories?" This poses me: I know fellows who could recollect a hundred. I know fellows, merely superficial, shallow men, who are never silent, who have a story or a joke for everything. I consider, "Let me see": I try to think of one. The beginnings of twenty stories occur to me mistily. Also the commencement of riddles as far as "Why is a—," or "When is a—," I've got some noted down in my pocket-book, if I could only get out of the room and refer to it quietly in the passage. I can't take it out before everybody; that's the worst of an artificial memory.

Happy Thought.—To read two pages of Macmillan's *Jest Book* every morning while dressing, committing at least one story to memory.

Childers proposes "Whist." I never feel certain of myself at whist: I point to the fact that there are four without me. Poss Felmyr says if I'll sit down he'll cut in presently. "I play?" I reply, "Yes, a little." I am Stenton's partner: Englefield and Childers are against us. Sixpenny points, shilling on the rub. Stenton says to me, "You'll score." Scoring always puzzles me. I know it's done with half a crown, a shilling, a sixpence, and a silver candlestick. Sometimes one bit of money is under the candlestick, sometimes two.

Happy Thought.—To watch Englefield scoring: soon pick it up again.

First Rubber.—Stenton deals: Childers is first hand, I'm second. Heart trumps: the Queen. It's wonderful how quick they are in arranging their cards. After I've sorted all mine carefully, I find a trump among the clubs. Having placed him in his position on the right of my hand, I find a stupid Three of Clubs among the spades: settled *him*. Lastly, a King of Diamonds upside down, which seems to entirely disconcert me; put *him* right. Englefield says, "Come, be quick": Stenton tells me "not to hurry myself." I say I'm quite ready, and wonder to myself what Childers will lead.

Childers leads the Queen of Clubs. I consider for a moment what is the duty of second hand; the word "finessing" occurs to me here. I can't recollect if putting on a three of the same suit is finessing: put on the three, and look at my partner to see how he likes it. He is watching the table. Englefield lets it go, my partner lets it go; the trick is Childers'. I feel that somehow it's lost through my fault. His lead again: spades. This takes me so by surprise that I have to rearrange my hand, as the spades have got into a lump. I have two spades, an ace and a five. Let me see, "If I play the five I —" I can't see the consequence. "If I play the ace it *must* win unless it's trumped." Stenton says in a deep voice, "Play away." The three look from one to the other. Being flustered, I play the ace: the trick is mine. I wish it was n't as I have to lead. I'd give something if I might consult Poss, who is behind me, or my partner. All the cards look ready for playing, yet I don't like to disturb them. Let me think what's been played already. Stenton asks me, "If I'd like to look at the last trick?" As this will give *me* time, and *them* the idea that I am following out my own peculiar tactics, I embrace the offer. Childers displays the last trick. I look at it. I say, "Thank you," and he shuts it up again. Immediately afterwards I can't recollect what the cards were in that trick: if I did it would n't help me. They are becoming impatient.

About this time somebody's Queen of Diamonds is taken. I was n't watching how the trick went, but I am almost certain it was fatal to the Queen of Diamonds; that is to say, if it *was* the Queen of Diamonds; but I don't like to ask. The next trick, which is something in spades, trumped by Englefield, I pass as of not much importance. Stenton growls, "Did n't I see that he 'd got no more spades in his hand." No, I own I did n't. Stenton, who is not an encouraging partner, grunts to himself. In a subsequent round, I having lost a trick by leading spades, Stenton calls out, "Why, did n't you see they were trumping spades?" I defend myself; I say I *did* see him, Englefield, trump *one* spade, but I thought that he had n't any more trumps. I say this as if I 'd been reckoning the cards as they 've been played.

Happy Thought.—Try to reckon them, and play by system next rubber.

I keep my trumps back till the last; they 'll come out and astonish them. They *do* come out and astonish *me*. Being taken by surprise

I put on my king when I ought to have played the knave, and both surrender to the ace and queen. I say, "Dear me, how odd!" I think I hear Stenton saying sarcastically in an undertone, "O yes; confoundedly odd." I try to explain, and he interrupts me at the end of the last deal but two by saying testily, "It's no use talking, if you attend, we may just save the odd."

Happy Thought.—Save the odd.

My friend, the Queen of Diamonds, who, I thought, had been played, and taken by some one or other at a very early period of the game, suddenly reappears out of my partner's hand, as if she were part of a conjuring trick. Second hand can't follow suit and can't trump. I think I see what he intends me to do here. I've a trump and a small club. "When in doubt," I recollect the infallible rule, "play a trump." I don't think any one expected this trump. Good play.

Happy Thought.—Trump. I look up diffidently; my partner laughs, so do the others.

My partner's is not a pleasant laugh. I can't help asking, "Why? isn't that right: it's ours?" "O yes," says my partner, sarcastically "it *is* ours." "Only," explains little Bob Englefield, "you've trumped your partner's best card."

I try again to explain that by *my* computation, the Queen of Diamonds had been played a long time ago. My partner won't listen to reason. He replies, "You might have *seen* that it wasn't." I return, "Well, it couldn't be helped, we'll win the game yet." This I add to encourage him, though, if it depends on *me*, I honestly (to myself) don't think we shall.

Happy Thought.—After all, we *do* get the odd trick. Stenton ought to be in a better humor, but he isn't; he says, "The odd! we ought to have been three." Englefield asks me how honors are? I don't know. Stenton says, "Why, you (meaning me) had two in your own hand." "O yes, I had." I'd forgotten it. "Honors easy," says Stenton to me. I agree with him. Now I've got to score with this confounded shilling, sixpence, half-crown, and a candlestick.

Happy Thought.—Ask Bob Englefield how *he* scores generally.

He replies, "O, the usual way," and as he does n't illustrate his meaning, his reply is of no use to me whatever. How can I find out without showing them that I don't know?

Happy Thought (*while* Childers *deals*).—Pretend to forget to score till next time. Englefield will have to do it, perhaps, next time, then watch Englefield. Just as I am arranging my cards from right to left—

Happy Thought.—To alternate the colors black and red, beginning this time with black (right) as spades are trumps. Also to arrange them in their rank and order of precedence. Ace on the right, if I've got one—yes—king next, queen next,—and the hand begins to look very pretty. I can quite imagine Whist being a fascinating game.—Stenton reminds me that I've forgotten to mark "one up."

Happy Thought.—Put sixpence by itself on my left hand. Stenton asks, "What's that for?"

Happy Thought.—To say it's the way I *always* mark.

Stenton says, "O, go on." I look round to see what we're waiting for, and Englefield answers me, "Go on, it's you; you're first hand." I beg their pardon. I must play some card or other and finish arranging my hand during the round. Anything will do to begin with. Here's a Two of Spades, a little one, on my left hand; throw him out.

"Hallo!" cries Englefield, second hand, "Trumps are coming out early." I quite forgot spades were trumps; that comes from that horrid little card being on the left instead of the right.

Happy Thought.—Not to show my mistake; nod at Englefield, and intimate that he'll see what's coming.

So, by the way, will my partner. In a polite moment I accept another cup of tea. I don't want it, and have to put it by the half-crown, shilling and candlestick on the whist-table, where I'm afraid of knocking it over, and am obliged to let it get quite cold as I have to attend to the game.

Happening to be taking a spoonful, with my eyes anxiously on the cards, when my turn comes, Stenton says, "*Do* play, never mind your tea." Whist brutalizes Stenton: what a pity!

Happy Thought.—Send this game, as a problem, to a Sporting Paper.

Happy Thought.—Why not write generally for Sporting papers?

Stenton says, "*Do* play!" I do.

Happy Thought.—Write a Treatise on Whist, so as to teach myself the game.

FINISHING THE RUBBER—NEW GAME—CONVERSATION.

We finish a second game, and Stenton says, "We win a single." This I am to score:

having some vague idea on the subject, I hide my half-crown under the candlestick. When our adversaries subsequently win a double, and there is some dispute about what we 've done before, I forget my half-crown under the candlestick, until asked rather angrily by Stenton if I did n't mark the single, when I am reminded by Poss Felmyr that I secreted the half-crown. This I produce triumphantly as a proof of a single.

Happy Thought. — Buy *Hoyle's Laws of Whist.* Every one ought to know how to mark up a single and a double.

I get very tired of whist after the second round of the third game. Wish I could feel faint, so that Poss Felmyr might take my place; or have a violent fit of sneezing which would compel me to leave the room.

Happy Thought.—If you give your mind to it, you can sneeze sometimes. I talk about draughts and sneezing, while Englefield deals. Englefield says, *apropos* of sneezing, that he knew a man who always caught a severe cold whenever he ate a walnut. If a fact: curious.

Old Mrs. Childers has woke up (she has been dozing by the fire with her knitting on the ground) and begins "to take notice," as they say of babies. She *will* talk to me: I can't attend to her and trumps at the same time. I think she says that she supposes I've a great deal of practice in whist-playing at the clubs. I say, "Yes; I mean, beg her pardon, no," and Stenton asks me, before taking up the trick, if I have n't got a heart, that being the suit I had to follow. I reply, "No," and my answer appears to disturb the game. On hearts coming up three hands afterwards, I find a two of that suit, which, being sticky, had clung to a Knave of Diamonds.

Happy Thought.—"Heart clinging to diamonds"; love yielding to the influence of wealth; or, by the way, *vice versa*, but good idea, somehow. Won't say it out, or they'll discover my revoke.

Happy Thought.—Keep the two until the end of the game, and throw it down among the rubbish at the end. I suppose the last cards which players always dash down don't count, and mine will go with them unobserved.

Happy Thought.—One act of duplicity necessitates another, just as one card will not stand upright by itself without another to support it. [Put this into "Moral Inversions," forming heading of Chapter 10, Book vi., Vol. xii. of *Typical Developments.* Must note this down to-night.]

The game is finishing. Luckily, our opponents have it all their own way, and suddenly, much to my surprise and relief, they show their hands and win, we only having made one trick.

Happy Thought.—Poss Felmyr takes my place.

On reckoning up I find that somehow or other I 've lost half a crown more than I expected. You can lose a good deal at sixpenny points. Stenton, who hears this remark made to Mrs. Childers, observes, "Depends how you play." I do not retort, as I am fearful about the subject of revoking coming up. *Moral Query.*—Was what I did with my Two of Hearts dishonesty or nervousness? Would n't it lead to cheating, to false dice, and ultimately to the Old Bailey? I put these questions to myself while eating a delicate piece of bread-and-butter handed to me by Mrs. Felmyr. I smile and thank her, even while these thoughts are in my bosom. Ah, Bob Englefield has no such stage for his dramas as the human bosom, no curtain that hides half as much from the spectators as a single-breasted waistcoat. More tea? thank you, yes.

Happy Thought.—Single-breasted waistcoat! Ah, who is single-breasted? Is that the fashion! [Note all this down in cipher in my book, "Moral Inversion" chapter, *Typical Developments.*]

I pick up old Mrs. Childers' knitting. I take this opportunity of saying, jocosely, that

I suppose that's what ladies call "dropping a stitch." No one hears it, except the old lady, who does n't understand it. I shall repeat this another day when they 're not playing cards, or talking together, as the ladies are.

Happy Thought.—To tell it as one of Sheridan's good things. Then they'll laugh.

Old Mrs. Childers says she thinks the moat's rising, and that the baker will have to come over in the punt. Childers, at the table, says : "Nonsense, mother." She appeals to me as to whether it is n't damp, and whether the rain won't make the moat rise? And do I think, from what I 've seen of it, that the punt is safe for the baker? Yes, I do think so. She observes that I 'm too young to have rheumatism, or suffer from cold in the ears. I don't know why I should feel offended at the old lady's remark, but I do. I feel inclined to say (rudely, if she was n't so old) that I 'm not too young, and have had the rheumatics: the latter proudly. She dares say I don't remember the flood there was in Leicestershire in 1812 ! No, I don't : "Was it bad?" I ask—not that I care, but I like to be respectful to old ladies. "Ah!" she replies, shaking her head slowly at the fire, as if it was *its* fault. I get nothing more out of her.

Mrs. Childers is working something for the children. Mrs. Poss asks about a peculiar sort of trimming for her dress. Mrs. Childers stops to explain, and point her remarks with the scissors. They are deep in congenial subjects, and don't mind me. No more does old Mrs. Childers, who has dropped her knitting, and is asleep again, quite upright, in her chair.

Happy Thought.—To ask the ladies to play on the piano.

It will disturb the game, Mrs. Childers thinks. Two of the players seem of the same opinion, but they 're losing, I discover. The two others are smiling, and would like a tune to enliven them. Childers calls out "Mother!" loudly, which makes the old lady wake with a start, and on finding that the moat has not risen and that the baker has n't come in the punt ("which she was dreaming of, curious enough," she says), she begs Mat not to call like that again, and I pick up her knitting for her. She thanks me, and asks if I recollect the great floods in Leicestershire in 1812. I reply, as I did before, that I don't. It leads to no information. Wonder how old she is?

She rises, and thinks, my dears, that it is time for Bedfordshire, which is her little joke; she gives it us every night at exactly the same time, and in exactly the same manner. It always commands a laugh. The ladies did n't know it was so late, and put up their work, hoping I'll excuse them not playing this evening. They're afraid I've found it very dull.

Happy Thought.—To say, " More dull when you're away." Just stopped in time, and turned it off with a laugh and a good night. I must have looked as if I was going to say something, as Mrs. Poss says, "What?" and I reply, "Oh, nothing," vaguely, and *she* laughs, and I laugh, and Mrs. Childers laughs, and says good night laughing, and old Mrs. Childers smiles and repeats her joke about Bedfordshire, which she evidently thinks we are all still laughing at, and this makes us all laugh again, and Stenton and Englefield, who, having lost, are fondly clinging to the whist-table, laugh as well, and saying good night becomes quite a hysterically comic piece of work, so much so that I wonder we don't all sit down in our chairs, or on the carpet (old Mrs. Childers on the carpet!) and have convulsions; and all this because I *did n't* say what I was going to say. They did n't laugh when I *did* make a really good joke this evening.

The ladies have gone. "Now," says Childers, "how about pipes and grogs?" Carried *nem. con.* Englefield proposes we stop whist and play Bolerum. What is Bolerum? Does n't any one know? Childers knows, it appears; he and Englefield will show it us: and to begin with, he and Englefield (this, they say, will simplify matters) will keep the bank.

The game, they explain, is very simple: so it appears. In fact its simplicity hardly seems to be its great charm to those who do not happen to be the bank. The players back their sixpences against the bank, and the bank wins. Childers calls it "a pretty game."

"One, two, three, four,—bank wins," cries Englefield; "pay up!" And we give him sixpence apiece.

"One, two, three, four, five,—bank again," cries Childers; "tizzies round," by which he means that we are again to subscribe sixpence apiece. Poss says, after five times of this, that he does n't see it. Stenton, the philosopher, taking a mathematical view of it, attempts to show how many chances there are in the players favor, but ends in demonstrating clearly that it is at least a hundred to one on the bank each time. This argument occupies a quarter of an hour, and three pieces of note paper, which Stenton covers with algebraic signs. Childers still sticks to it, that "it's a pretty game." We admit that it is very pretty, but we get up from the table. What game shall we play? We decide (and sixpences are at the bottom of our decision), "None."

"Quite cold," observes Stenton. We gather in front of the fire.

Poss suddenly wonders that I've not yet seen the ghost in my room. Childers says "Ah," and then we all stare at the fire, wondering at nothing : silence.

Childers turns quietly to Englefield, and inquires, "if he knows Jimmy Flewter?" Englefield does. Childers asks "if he heard about his row with Menzies?" Englefield, with his pipe in his mouth, and embracing his knee, nods assent. "It's settled," says Childers, and stares at the fire again. "Foolish of him," observes Poss. "Very," says Stenton, in his deep bass. It would be rude to ask who Flewter is, but this sort of conversation is very irritating.

Childers anticipates me by saying, "You don't know Jimmy Flewter?" I do not, but signify I am ready to hear anything to his advantage or disadvantage for the sake of conversation.

"Ah, then," returns Childers, "you would n't enjoy the story."

"Must know the man," puts in Stenton, "to enjoy the story." Poss assents, and smiles as if at a reminiscence. They all chuckle to themselves. I wish I had a story to chuckle over to *myself*. I wish I knew Flewter.

"Seen my lord, to-day?" asks Englefield of Childers. Wonder who "My lord" is.

"No, comes to-morrow," is the answer.

"Paint?" asks Poss. "Sketch," answers Childers.

"Odd fish," observes Bob Englefield, putting on his spectacles to wind up his watch. "Very," says Poss. We knock out our ashes, and, finishing our grog, go to bed.

Happy Thought.—Shall find out who "My lord" is to-morrow. Hang Flewter! Rain, violent: no ghost. Room seems darker. Window troublesome. Think of Fridoline. Wish it was Valentine's Day, I 'd send her a sonnet. Too sleepy to think of it now. * * * Jimmy Flewter. * * *

F. C. BURNARD.

EDWARD EVERETT AT THE COURT OF ST. JAMES.*

A RECENT statement that a newly nominated minister to England did not play any game at cards reminded the Easy Chair of a little incident which it remembered to have heard related by one of the most accomplished of our foreign ministers—Edward Everett. Mr. Everett's accomplishments were different from those of an American minister who was once sent to the Court of France, and of whom an admiring *attaché* remarked, with enthusiasm, that he could "smoke and chew perfectly at the same time." Presumptively the same gentleman could play an excellent game at whist. But this, as Mr. Everett said, was very much more

* By the courtesy of George William Curtis.

than he could do. According to the story, Mr. Everett was to present his credentials to the Queen on the same day with the presentation of the Italian Minister, and repaired at the proper hour, in the costume of ceremony, to the palace, where he found his Italian colleague, also officially and splendidly arrayed. The presentation took place in due form, and the ministers having been bidden to dinner, were informed by the Prime Minister that the Duchess of Kent, the Queen's mother, desired them to join her in a game of whist.

"I am sorry for either of you who may be my partner," said the Prime Minister, smiling, as he rose to lead the way to the Duchess, "for I know very little about the game."

As they passed along, Mr. Everett turned to his diplomatic companion, and said, with lofty urbanity: "I also must entreat your Excellency's forbearance if you should have the misfortune to be allotted to me as a partner, for I have very little practice in the game." The Italian Excellency bowed courteously, and gravely assured the American Minister that the necessity of forbearance was mutual, for he also had very little acquaintance with the game. The Duchess received her guests with all ceremony, and having indicated who was to be her partner, the three dignified personages who were not very familiar with whist seated themselves, and the game was about to begin, when a lady of honor placed herself by the chair of the Duchess, who graciously remarked to her companions: "Your Excellencies will excuse me, but, to prevent embarrassment to you, I have requested this lady to prompt me, as, indeed, I am not very familiar with the game." The Excellencies bowed profoundly, and the ceremonial game of whist proceeded.

Se non è vero, è ben trovato. Mr. Everett had a keen sense of humor, and he said that in all his official life he had seen nothing more absurd than that game. He was an excellent story-teller, and the narrative lost nothing in the telling that Washington Irving was one of the amused listeners. The recent Congressional debate upon diplomatic appropriations revealed the fact that there is a great deal of this kind of dummy whist in diplomatic life, a great deal of playing at playing at cards, solemnly and in fine clothes. It is perhaps no serious disadvantage to an American minister that he is not an accomplished whist-player, nor even an expert in simultaneous smoking and chewing. The Easy Chair has seen in other years an American minister driving through the streets of a great city, during a festival, with one leg hanging over the side of an open carriage, and a cigar protruding from his mouth at the familiar Bowery angle. Within the range of the same memory another American minister stood in the balcony of a hotel in the costume of the King of the Cannibal Islands, haranguing the wondering crowd in the street with the tearful pathos of Senator Dilworthy. Still another received two American ladies by appointment in his chamber at an inn in the morning, wearing his hat, and with a half-emptied bottle of whiskey standing upon the table. Expressive silence may muse the moral. But it is pertinent for the Easy Chair, which deals with the minor morals and manners, to suggest that they should always be reckoned as necessary parts of the outfit of every American minister, as indeed, they conspicuously have been in the instance of Mr. Everett himself and some of his illustrious successors.

GEORGE WILLIAM CURTIS,
in "Editor's Easy Chair," *Harper's Monthly Magazine.*

METTERNICH'S WHIST.

BE sure, too, that the pursuit of this enchanting game does not tempt you to neglect your duties in other respects. Do all your work thoroughly before you sit down. Without putting the matter upon higher ground, there is nothing that injures an honest man's game more than the reflection that he has left a duty unfulfilled; his conscience whisks away his attention, and his money and his temper are then pretty sure to follow. Whist embittered the death-bed of the great Metternich.

Fifteen years before his death, that great statesman knew little of the wondrous game, as full of wiles and stratagems as his own crafty mind.

I was walking with him at that period in a gallery of his own house at Vienna, and through an open door we perceived some ladies of his family playing at whist.

"That is a game," remarked he, "only fit for women and fools."

I smiled and shook my head.

"I have played whist for fifty years, I tell you," continued the prince, a little heated by my pantomimic contradiction, "and I think I am capable of forming an opinion."

"You have played *something* for fifty years, prince," returned I, pityingly, "but you never played whist in your life."

The astute Austrian was so struck with the audacious confidence of my assertion, that he submitted to become my pupil in the science.

I do not say that he surpassed his tutor, for that would be gross flattery; but he very soon *un*learned what he knew, and got to play a most admirable game. He threw himself into the new art with his accustomed energy, and soon became passionately attached to it. Years afterwards an express arrived with despatches for him from Galicia and found him engaged at his favorite game.

He placed the papers on the mantel-piece and went on playing throughout that night and far into the morning. When the party broke up he was horrified to discover that upon his immediate reply depended the fate of two thousand persons.

The infamous "Galician Massacre" would never have taken place if Metternich had not loved whist "not wisely, but too well."

Chamber's Journal.

LORD LYTTON AS A WHIST-PLAYER.

LORD LYTTON was very fond of whist, and he and I both belonged to the well-known Portland Club, in which were to be found many of the celebrated players of the day. He never showed the slightest disposition of a gambler. He played the game well, and without excitement or temper, and apparently his whole attention was concentrated upon it; but it was curious to see that at every interval that occurred in the rubbers he would rush off to a writing-table, and with equally concentrated attention proceed with some literary work until called again to take his place at the whist-table. There was a member of the club, a very harmless, inoffensive man, of the name of Townend, for whom Lord Lytton entertained a mortal antipathy, and would never play whist while that gentleman was in the room. He firmly believed that he brought him bad luck. I was witness to what must be termed an odd coincidence. One afternoon, when Lord Lytton was playing, and had enjoyed an uninterrupted run of luck, it suddenly turned, upon which he exclaimed, "I am sure that Mr. Townend has come into the club." Some three minutes after, just time enough to ascend the stairs, in walked this unlucky personage. Lord Lytton, as soon as the rubber was over, left the table and did not renew the play.

SERJEANT BALLANTINE'S
Experiences of a Barrister's Life.

SOME LITERARY RECOLLECTIONS.*

* * * For the last five-and-twenty years of my life I have only had three days of consecutive holiday once a year; while all the year round (from another necessity of the pen) the Sundays have been as much working-days with me as the week-days.

Such from-day-to-day labors, though not, it is true, extending to long hours, would perhaps have been impossible but for the relief afforded by some favorite amusement. This, in my case, as it has been in that of much greater men, has been the noble game of whist, which I have played regularly, for two or three hours a day, for the last thirty years. It does not, indeed, much matter what it is, so that the relaxation is an attractive one, but I pity that man from the

* By permission of Messrs. Harper & Brothers.

bottom of my heart who can find no interest in a game. It is not every one who, like Sarah Battle, can relax their minds over a book, and least of all those who write books. I have noticed that those of my own calling who read the most are not the best students of human nature, and fall most often into the pit of plagiarism. How often have I heard it said—too late—by those who have most certainly earned their play-time: "How I wish I had an amusement!" The taste for such things must be caught early (like the measles) and indulged (like the patient).

What position, for example, is more unsatisfactory than that of the man who has only played whist occasionally—say once a week—and " makes up a rubber to oblige "?

In a partner's eyes, at least, such a person will never meet his obligations. Mackworth Praed must have been a whist-player, or he never could have depicted *Quince:*

> " Some public principles he had,
>   But was no flatterer nor fretter;
> He rapped his box when things were bad
>   And said, ' I cannot make them better.'

> And much he loathed the patriots' snort,
> And much he scorned the placeman's snuffle,
> And cut the fiercest quarrel short
> With 'patience, gentlemen, and shuffle.'"

Men of letters are rarely good card-players—Lord Lytton and Lever are almost the only exceptions I can call to mind,—but some of them have been fond of whist, and have enlivened it by their sallies. A few of these, which I have happened myself to hear, seem worthy of record.

A guest being asked to a dinner-party, which was to precede an evening at cards, thus apologized for coming in morning costume: "The suit is surely no matter, so long as one is a trump."

A man who had his foot on a gout-rest was holding very bad cards, and complaining alike of his luck and his malady. Upon being reproached by his more fortunate adversary for his irritation, he suddenly exclaimed: "It's all very well for *you*, but a 'game hand' is a very different thing from a 'game leg.'"

On another occasion the same gentleman (whose temper, gout or no gout, was always a little short), jumped up from the seat where he had been losing and declared that he would play no more. "But you'll break up the table," pleaded the others pathetically. "If it is broken up there will still be three 'legs' left," was his uncompromising reply.

A whist-player, who, even though a loser, ought to have known better than to have jested upon such a tender subject, once remarked, in reference to the considerable number of novels for which I have been responsible: "Nobody can deny, my dear fellow, that you have great 'numerical strength.'"

I remember a little poem called *Dumby*, written by a brother novelist, who has himself, alas! left a vacant place at the four-square table forever, which has a pathetic singularity about it:

> "I see the face of the friend I lost
>   Before me as I sit,
>   His thin white hands, so subtle and swift,
>   And his eyes that gleam with wit.
>
> "I see him across the square green cloth
>   That's dappled with black and red;
>   Between the luminous globes of light
>   I watch the friend long dead.

"It is only I who can see him there,
　With victory in his glance,
As, the cross ruff stopped, he strides along
　Like Wellington through France.

"He died years past in the jungle reeds,
　But still I see him sit,
Facing me with his fan of cards,
　And those eyes that beam with wit."

JAMES PAYN.

ANECDOTES FROM CAVENDISH'S CARD-TABLE TALK.

WHEN my book on whist was first published the authorship was kept a profound secret. I sent a copy, "with the author's compliments," to my father, and great was the amusement of my brother (who knew all about it) and myself at the "Governor's" guesses as to where it could have come from.

One evening, when about to play a family rubber for love, we proposed to the "Governor" to play one of the hands in the book, "to see if the fellow knew anything about it." He consented. We sorted one of the hands (Hand No. xxxvi., p. 246, 12th edition), giving my father Y's hand, others of our circle taking the other hands, and my brother sitting out book in hand, to see whether we followed the "book" play.

The "Governor" played the hand all right till he came to the coup at trick 9, when he went on with his established diamonds.

Frater. (interrupting).—The book says that is wrong.

Pater.—Well, what does the book say?

Frater.—The book says you should lead a trump.

Pater.—But there are no more trumps in! (Hesitates, and seeing that he has two trumps, and that leading one of them will not do any harm, leads it, and then turns round triumphantly and says): Now what does the book say?

Frater (very quietly).—The book says you should lead *another* trump.

This was too much. Lead a thirteenth trump when you can give your partner a discard! Oh! no! So the "Governor" would not and did not lead the trump, and he scored four.

We then persuaded him to play the hand again, and to lead the thirteenth trump. To his surprise he scored five.

He then admitted it was "very good," but could not think who in the world had sent him that book.

Clay told me that when he first played whist at a London club he was horrified to see an old gentleman deliberately looking over one of his adversaries' hands. Mr. Pacey, the player whose hand was overlooked, was, as it happened, an old friend of Clay's, and, the rubber being over, Clay took an immediate opportunity of advising him to hold up his hand when playing against P——, adding :

"The last hand he saw every card you held."

"Oh! no! he did n't!" replied Mr. Pacey, who was well aware of P——'s peculiarities, "he only saw a few I put in the corner to puzzle him."

CAVENDISH'S *Card-Table Talk*.

ADVANTAGE OF SKILL AT WHIST.

IN the latter part of the winter of 1857, during an after-dinner conversation, it was remarked by some of the party that whist is a mere matter of chance, since no amount of ingenuity can make a king win an ace, and so on. This produced an argument as to the merits of the game; and, as two of the disputants obstinately maintained the original position, it was proposed to test their powers by matching them against two excellent players in the room. To this match, strange to say, the bad players agreed, and a date was fixed. Before the day arrived it was proposed to play the match in double, another rubber of two good against two bad players being formed in an adjoining room, and the hands being played over again, the good players having the cards previously held by the bad ones, and *vice versa*, the order of the play being, of course, in every other respect preserved. The difficulty now was to find two players sufficiently bad for this purpose; but two men were found, on condition of having odds laid them at starting, which was accordingly done.

On the appointed day a table was formed in room A, and as soon as the first hand was played, the cards were re-sorted and conveyed into room B. There the hand was played over again, the good players in room B having the cards that the bad players had in room A. At the end of the hand the result was noted for comparison, independently of the score, which was conducted in the usual way. Thirty-three hands were played in each room. In room A the good players held very good cards, and won four rubbers out of six; in points, a balance of eighteen. In room B the good players had, of course, the bad cards. They played seven rubbers, with the same number of hands that in the other room had played six, and they won three out of the seven, losing seven points on the balance. The difference, therefore, was eleven points, or nearly one point a rubber in favor of skill.

A comparison of tricks only showed some curious results. In seven of the hands the score by cards in each room was the same. In eighteen hands the balance of the score by cards was in favor of the superior players; in eight hands in favor of the inferior. In one of these hands the bad players won two by cards at one table, and three by cards at the other.

The most important result is that at both tables the superior players gained a majority of tricks. In room A they won on the balance nineteen by tricks; in room B they won two by tricks.

It will be observed that this experiment does not altogether eliminate luck, as bad play sometimes succeeds. But by far the greater part of luck, *viz.*, that due to the superiority of winning cards, is, by the plan described, quite got rid of.

Dr. Pole (the *Field*, June 16, 1866) arrives at nearly the same result by a statistical method. He writes to this effect:

"It is very desirable to ascertain the value of skill at whist.

"The voluntary power we have over results at whist is compounded of—1. The system of play.—2. The personal skill employed."

The modern system, which combines the hands of the two partners, as against no system (the personal skill of all being pretty equal), is worth—Dr. Pole thinks—about half a point a rubber, or rather more. About nine hundred rubbers played by systematic against old-fashioned players gave a balance of nearly five hundred points in favor of system.

The personal skill will vary with each individual, and is difficult to estimate; but, looking at published statistics, in which Dr. Pole had confidence, he puts the advantage of a very superior player (all using system) at about a quarter of a point a rubber; consequently the advantage due to combined personal skill (*i. e.*, two very skilful against two very unskilful players, all using system), would be more than half a point a rubber.

The conclusion arrived at by Dr. Pole is that "the total advantage of both elements of power over results at Whist may, under very favorable circumstances, be expected to amount to as much as one point per rubber."

Now, at play-clubs, nearly all the players adhere more or less closely to system, and the great majority have considerable personal skill. Consequently, only the very skilful player can expect to win anything, and he will only have the best player at the table for a partner, on an average, once in three times. It follows from this that the expectation of a very skilful player at a play-club will only average, at the most say a fifth or a sixth of a point a rubber.

CAVENDISH'S *Card-Table Talk*.

SOME WHIST CHAT.

A FEW months ago an essay of mine on the American card game, poker, appeared in these pages. I have been since told by Americans, with that frankness which is so engaging a quality of theirs, that though I may be able to calculate to a nicety the chances of the various poker hands, and those on which the drawing of fresh cards at poker depends, I should be everlastingly beaten if I played at poker in America. I think it exceedingly likely, for poker is not a game at which I have ever played. I shall probably escape crushing defeat at the game, because I am never likely to play it. It is a game expressly invented for betting purposes, and betting has always seemed to me a foolish and degrading habit; so that I am not likely to find myself at the same table with American poker-players. Moreover, if newspaper notes do them justice, some of the most successful exponents of the game in America modify their chances by manipulative processes which I had not taken into account in my poker essay. The chance of a hand with four aces, for example, is by no means what is indicated in that essay if the dealer is able by dexterity of hand to deal himself any cards he may please. In the company of ordinary players, again, a full hand is doubtless a very good hand to stand on, but a man of guileless type would be wise not to stand on a hand even of four kings if he found a dexterous opponent putting money down heavily, lest it should presently appear that the four kings had been dealt him specially to make him wager freely by an opponent who had at the same time dealt himself four aces or a straight flush. Such things have been; and it is by no means uncommon in some parts of America for a man to lay down with a sigh, a hand of four knaves, queens, or kings (face downwards be it understood, lest he should be shot for the implied suspicion, even though four aces should lie under the shooter's hand). It is even said, I know not with what degree of truth, that in some Western States you must not be unduly pained if you should find four aces beaten by five jacks; still less must you question whether five jacks belong naturally to a normal pack.

What a relief it is to turn from a game like poker, associated with greed and lying bluster and brag, to the noble game which every Englishman loves (though few play it well)—the best if not the oldest of card games—whist! It is played indeed for money, as poker is; but with what a difference! At poker the money is everything; no one would think of playing at the game except to win or lose money; at whist, the chief reason why money is staked is that the game may be well and truly played. No true lover of whist would like to hear such stories of money lost and won at whist as are told of exciting poker games. The author of *Guy Livingstone*, in his *Belle Dame sans Merci*, introduces a story originally told about the skilful whist-player James Clay, which seems to imply that many fortunes have been lost by bad whist play. A partner of Clay's had lost a game by leading from a plain suit, though holding five trumps, one honor. At the close of the hand he asked Clay (who loved him not) whether a trump lead would not have been wiser. "It is computed," slowly and gravely answered the great whist-player, "that eleven thousand men, once heirs to fair fortunes, are now wandering abroad in a state of destitution because they would not lead trumps from five, one honor." But either Clay was savage at the foolish play of his partner, in which case a man will say anything, or he purposely Americanized the truth, which, correctly expressed, would have been less amusing and effective. For where would have been the interest of such a rejoinder as this? "It is computed that by failing to take the chance of a great game which the possession of five trumps, one honor gives you and your partner, you lose about one point out of $23\frac{2}{11}$ of those which, but for this fault of play, you would have made in the course of a sufficiently long run; supposing 2,318 points lost and as many won each year (a very fair allowance of play), but for this fault, then 2,218 only would be won and 2,418 lost, a balance of 200 to the bad, by a player who committed the fault into which you have just fallen, partner. At a sovereign each, which is higher play than I recommend for neophytes like you, you would probably lose £200 per annum. But then (also probably) you would correct the fault of play before the year was out. However, we must not keep the table waiting. Mr. Vincent Flemyng, it is your turn to deal."

It is singular that, being so fine a game as it is, whist should be so little known. I have just said, indeed, that every one in England loves whist. I should have said that every one loves a game which is supposed to be whist. But ninety-nine out of a hundred of those who suppose they play whist hardly know what the game is. The game at which they really play has been called by the ingenious Pembridge "bumblepuppy." It is a sort of a blunder-blindfold game, which must be interesting, I suppose, since so many play it. Nay, let us be honest. Even we who know what whist is (which is by no means claiming to play finely) have most of us had a period of bumblepuppy. Can we not remember how we sat gravely down to what we called whist? When our hands were delivered to us, we set down in our minds each ace as a card to be led at the first opportunity. We had little fear about our kings, for we knew that the aces over them would be led out by the other players just as frankly as we should lead out our own. Even queens had a fair chance. But the single card was our chief delight. That was led out at once, and so our little trumps were safely made; for no one would think of leading out trumps while there seemed to be a chance of using any in ruffing. Somehow, a trick made by ruffing seemed worth two made in any other way. If no chance came for a ruff, trumps were reserved to the last. But even then our game retained its beautiful simplicity of character. The ace came out first, then in due order the king and the queen. To have led a small card from ace, queen, and others, would have seemed wild audacity, which might indeed succeed at times, but was too imprudent to be encouraged.

This game, however, the whist of the home circle and of Western America (in the Eastern States many Americans know true whist "real well"), is not whist at all. It owes its interest solely to chance. A player of this bumblepuppy game, who has been lucky in getting a number of good hands, does indeed arrogate to himself the character of a good player. He seems to regard his luck as something due to personal influence. Indeed, oddly enough, while a good whist-player, even if, with a good partner, he has to play against two bumblepuppy players, will never be assured of success, knowing how uncertain the chances are, you will generally find one of these know-nothings boasting confidently that he will win. Another way of recognizing the whist duffers is by their manner when the cards favor them. A good player, when he and his partner have made five or six by cards, will not be loudly jubilant, though, touching on the help received from the cards, he may congratulate his partner on some successful stroke of strategy; but the player of bumblepuppy, when he and his partner, having all the honors, and five out of six of the remaining high cards, have won the odd trick and so made a treble, will say: "He knew they would win," "He always does win," and otherwise take credit for a success which not even the skill of a Deschapelles could have managed to avert.

But though domestic whist, or bumblepuppy, has "these violent delights" for its exponents, it is not a game worth playing or talking about.

Majora canamus!

What is the real game of whist then, the reader may ask, if domestic whist is not whist at all? Is not the object the same? No doubt it is. The object of whist is to secure as many tricks as possible. High cards tell at whist as at bumblepuppy (I thank thee, Pembridge, for teaching me that word!) Nay, in quite a number of hands, luck tells as much at one game as at the other, and if the whist player is of sordid mind, as many are, he rejoices at the dull hands in which he has only had to play out winning cards as much as the veriest duffer of domestic whist at the way in which aces and kings take tricks. But whist is a game of science, a game calling for the exercise of keen perception, watchfulness, memory, patience and trust in the established laws of probability. It may sound like exaggeration to say that whist is far better calculated to develop the mind than many things taught at school, yet many a man can perceive a real gain to his mental qualities from whist practice, who would find it hard to recognize any good which he has obtained from learning how to write Latin verses with due attention to the niceties of the *cæsura*. A course of whist play is a capital way of training the memory, the powers of attention, and the temper; but nine boys out of ten gain nothing from a course of practice in determining the greatest common measures and the least common multiples of algebraical quantities.

Indeed, many of our best whist-players are complaining that whist is becoming too full of points requiring to be noticed and kept in the memory. A system has come into existence within the last thirty or forty years by which a player can convey information to his partner in various ways; and it is urged that instead of giving their minds to points of whist strategy, players now have to be constantly looking out for this signal or that indication. Many of the old players determine to have nothing to do with all this signalling; but, alas for them! they have no choice. It is too strong for them. Though they may never signal themselves; though they may resolutely decline to respond to any signal made by their partner, they *must* notice the signals alike of their partner and of the adversaries, or all sorts of disasters will happen, for which their partners will properly hold them responsible. Thus, a player signals for trumps, and presently his partner responds by leading him a trump. Suppose now one of the other players has failed to notice the signal. He falls naturally into the mistake of supposing that the player who has led trumps is strong in them and that the other adversary is presumably weak. Under this mistake he presently forces what he supposes to be the strong trump hand, but in reality enables the weak hand to make trumps which would otherwise have fallen idle. Or, on the other hand, having a chance of forcing the strong trump hand, the player who has failed to notice the signal refrains religiously from doing so, imagining that he would be helping the enemy instead of cutting down his trump strength. Under these circumstances, partner, if of the reproachful sort, can rebuke much more effectively than where his own signal has merely been revoked. To the reproach, "Why did you not lead me a trump when I signalled?" there is always the ready answer, "I saw your signal, and I declined to respond to it, because I object to the signalling system." But what answer can be made when your partner says, "My good sir, you played the enemy's game? there was Y signalling for trumps, and you deliberately forced Z, giving him just the trick which made their game; or you failed to force Y, though that was the only way to save our game." You cannot answer that you saw the signal, but preferred to sacrifice the game rather than act upon it. You are obliged to tell the truth (and what could be more painful?) that you had failed to notice the enemy's signal.

Whist—the real game of whist, I mean—derives its interest entirely from strategy, by which either tricks are made by cards which would not, but for such strategy, have power to take those tricks, or by which the plans of the adversaries to achieve such ends are detected and foiled. Tricks may be made by high cards, but there is no interest in that. Any one can take a trick with the ace of trumps. Tricks may be made by finesse—that is, by playing, instead of the best card, a lower card, which may or may not take the trick according as the intermediate card or cards lie to the right or left. This is better; but the finesse pure and simple is a matter of mere chance, and so far as the actual gain of a trick is concerned there is no more scientific joy in the success of a finesse than in the capture of a trick by a high card. There is science in the finesse; but the scientific interest does not depend on the direct success or failure of the finesse at the moment, but on its bearing upon the general play of the hand. Again, tricks may be made by trumping winning cards of plain suits. There is often good science in bringing this about properly, not by the coarse lead of a single card or from a two-card suit, but by so arranging matters that the ruff, when made, shall not impair, but utilize the trump strength which lies between you and your partner. Special pleasure is there in the cross-ruff when ingeniously secured and properly employed; still more pleasure in tempting the enemy to a cross-ruff, which, while not lasting long enough to give them more than three or four tricks, just destroys their superior trump strength. But the great delight of whist strategy lies in the manœuvres by which small cards are made to conquer large ones, as when a long suit is successfully brought in, or the enemy forced by skilful strategy to lead up to a tenace. Nor is there less pleasure in noting and foiling the plans of the adversary for achieving these same ends. Nay, to the true player there ought to be pleasure even in noting the skill by which the enemy achieves success; but I fear me this is more than most players of whist attain to, however earnest may be their whist enthusiasm.

Of course chance has its part even in scientific whist. In playing 30,000 rubbers one of the finest living players of the game lost nearly 15,000, gaining only a balance of about 600 rubbers. Among the thousands of rubbers, a goodly proportion must have been lost against bad play and by the sheer influence of cards, that is, of chance. There must be some villainous whist-players living who can boast that they have played several rubbers against this fine player and won every rubber they played. Then, again, there is such a thing as good cards being beaten by sheer bad luck. Thus, there is that famous hand in which the Duke of Cumberland held ace, king, queen, and knave, in one plain suit; ace, king, queen in another; ace, king, in the third; while in trumps he held king, knave, nine, and seven; yet with this perfectly magnificent hand and the lead, leading also quite correctly, he did not make a single trick. Yet, although chance thus plays an important part in whist, and is, indeed, regarded by many as the element which gives to whist its great interest, the game even in its partial dependence on chance is a scientific one. Only science can answer the questions which the chance element introduces. Only science can avail to get the best results which the different components of the hands leave open to a player and his partner. When to scientific acumen are added a good memory, a careful and attentive mind, readiness in observation, brilliance of conception and aptitude in execution, we get the elements of fine play. But it is not true of the whist-player that he is born, not made. Practice alone can combine these elements to form a really fine player.

Chance, indeed, in whist causes good play often to fail and bad play to succeed. This is little understood by bad players. They judge only by immediate results, and if a sound rule leads to disaster, as must inevitably happen in a certain proportion of cases to which it is applied, they vow that the rule is a bad one, and are apt thenceforth to follow the unsound converse rule. For instance, it may be shown that in a majority of cases leading a small card from ace, three small ones, will be successful, the ace taking the second trick and the two first tricks going far to clear the suit. But sometimes this sound lead turns out badly. Your partner holds, perhaps, the queen, fourth player the fourchette to the queen—*i.e.*, knave, king; the first trick falls to the king, your ace is trumped second round and when trumps are exhausted the holder of the knave is found to have two more of the suit, both of which he makes, besides the knave (and the king which he had made the first round) or four tricks in the suit, besides the trick made by the ruff on your ace. This is rough on the sound lead, and some players can never forget such a *contretemps*. They forthwith adopt the system of leading the ace first from a suit of four to the ace. Now, in this case, there is really something to be said in favor of the ace lead, which is adopted on the Continent. The balance of advantages in favor of the small card lead is not heavy. Still the odds are in its favor. Now, suppose there were a teetotum with eleven faces, six marked with an A, five with a Z, and a small bet depended on the selection of the face which would come uppermost. Any one who wagered on the A systematically would be bound to win in the long run of many trials. If there were 1,100 trials he would be right about 600 times and wrong about 500 times, or would gain about 100 times the amount of his wager. In 11,000 trials he would be still more certain that he would win his wager by about one-eleventh of the total number of trials. Yet he would lose a number of times. It would often happen that he would lose ten or twelve times in succession. If he had been assured that the rule given to him was a sound one, but had not been allowed to look at the teetotum, and it so chanced that his first ten trials were all, or most of them unfavorable, it would be natural for him to begin to doubt whether the rule were really sound. But if the teetotum were shown to him, and he found there were six A faces to only five B faces, with an equal chance of any one of these faces showing, he would certainly be unwise to give up the sound A selection and adopt the unsound Z selection merely because it had happened that a few chance trials had given results unfavorable to the better choice. Now this is precisely what those whist players do who reject sound for unsound play, because sound play has occasionally turned out badly.

But, of course, it must happen in a certain proportion of cases that the right lead turns out unluckily. In two cases out of three the king falls to the enemy's ace, and the short-sighted seeing no farther, thinks this proves the lead to be bad. But even in the further play of the suit the result may be unfortunate. From a rough computation which I have made, I find reason to conclude that leading king from king, queen, and two others turns out well in about five cases out of nine. If my computation is right (the difficulty lies in taking into account the multitudinous varieties of arrangement outside the suit), then the lead turns out ill in four cases out of nine. Depend upon it, cavillers will pay much more attention to those four ninths of all the cases in which the lead fails than to the cases, though twenty-five per cent. more numerous, in which the lead turns out well. But, of course, the sound whist-player systematically adopts the lead which will turn out well in the majority of cases; he would do so even though the odds in his favor were not more than 101 to 100.

In the course of the reasoning just given, I have touched on the chance that a suit will go round such and such a number of times. Most of the rules for leading at whist depend on this particular chance, the calculation of which is easy enough, so far as principles are concerned, though laborious in practice. The whist-player cannot conveniently run through these calculations while the rest of the table wait for him to play. But rules of play, based either upon calculation or on long practice leading to the same conclusions, should be adopted systematically, as bound to be best in the long run. Of course, circumstances alter cases. Among the forty games I have collected in *How to Play Whist*, there is one in which that fine player, Mr. F. G. Lewis, ran counter to two rules in the very first card he played (the opening lead): having five trumps, he did not lead a trump, and leading from a plain suit of five cards headed by the ace he led the lowest but one (the customary lead when the suit is not headed by the ace) instead of the ace, the usual and generally the best lead. But that was because a higher rule overrode both those other rules—*viz.*, the rule that you should play to win.

I proceed to state some of the chances of particular arrangements of the cards in a particular hand, or of the cards of any suits in different hands. I shall not, as I did in my essay on poker, indicate the reasoning by which the various results have been obtained, for that reasoning was found rather difficult by those unacquainted with the methods of calculation considered, while those acquainted with the laws of combination can reason out the matter, I have no doubt, for themselves.

SOME OF THE CHANCES OF WHIST.

There are no less than 635,013,559,600 ways in which a hand can be made. That all the cards in the hand may be trumps (the dealer's of course, must be taken), the chance is but one in 158,753,389,900 (one fourth of the number just mentioned). A few years ago (see "Whist Whittling," in *How to Play Whist*, pp. 190, 191) two cases of the kind were recorded, and many seemed to suppose that there must be something wrong in the mathematical computation of the chance. For, they said, in 158,753,389,900 cases only one would give this particular hand, and yet two cases occurred within a few years of each other, within which time so many hands could not possibly have been dealt. Now there was here, at starting, the fallacy that because but one case in so many is favorable, so many trials must be made to give an even chance of the event occurring. As a matter of fact, a much smaller number of trials is necessary to give an even chance. Take a simple case—the tossing of a coin. Here there are two possible results, but it does not take two trials to give an even chance of tossing head—one trial suffices for that; and the chance of tossing head once at least in two trials instead of being one half is three fourths; the odds are not even, but three to one in favor of tossing a head. In like manner, if 158,753,389,900 hands were dealt, the odds are not even, but largely in favor of a hand of thirteen trumps being among them. Moreover, if the odds were shown to be ten or even twenty to one against the event occurring in a much smaller given number of trials, yet there is nothing very surprising in an event occurring when the odds against it are ten or twenty to one. But large though the number just mentioned may seem, the number of whist-players is also large. It would not be much out of the way to suppose that among all the whist-playing nations of the earth a million whist parties play *per diem*, and to each we may fairly assign twenty deals. On this assumption it would require only 7,950 days or not much more than twenty years, to give 159,000,000,000 trials, or much more than an even chance of the remarkable hand in question. Then, too, there are cases where the trumps are more likely to be distributed to one hand than if the distribution were absolutely at random. Thus suppose a cross-ruff has been established in a game, and five or six tricks taken that way; then it can readily happen that the five or six trumps which have thus fallen take the same position in each of the five or six tricks gathered by the same player. Suppose such a thing to happen, with five trumps only, once in a thousand games. Then it can be shown that the chance of the remaining cards of that suit all falling into the same hand is one in 2,629,575, making the chance of both events coming off, and all thirteen cards falling into one hand, one in 2,629,575,000, or the odds only 2,629,574,999 to 1 (instead of 158,753,389,899 to 1) against all thirteen trumps being in one hand. Large even as these odds are, the real odds must be much larger; otherwise, with the great number of whist hands constantly being dealt, we should hear of all-trump hands two or three times a year at least.

Turn now from this very rare hand to the arrangements which occur most frequently. It then might seem as though the commonest of all arrangements would be the one by which the cards are distributed most uniformly among the suits—*i. e.*, four of one suit, and three of each of the other suits. But this is not the case. In one sense, indeed, this is the commonest kind of hand. If you take a given suit—say clubs, for the four-card suit—then there are 16,726,464,040 possible arrangements, giving four clubs, three hearts, three diamonds and three spades; and there are not so many arrangements for any hand in which each particular suit is assigned a particular number of cards. But as the four-card suit can be chosen in four different ways, we get 66,905,856,160 possible arrangements of a hand with four of one suit and three of each of the others. Now, taking a hand with four of each of two suits, three of another, and two of the fourth suit, we find that if we assign definite suits for the three cards and for the two cards—say we have three hearts and two diamonds in each hand—there are only 11,404,-

407,300 possible arrangements giving four clubs, three hearts, three spades and two diamonds. This is considerably less than the number giving four clubs, three hearts, three spades, and three diamonds, to which, as a special arrangement for those suits, it comes next in frequency. But, instead of having only four ways in which to distribute our suits, we now have twelve. We can have any one of the four suits for our two-card suit, and combine with any one of the three remaining suits for our three-card suit, giving four times three, or twelve, possible ways of distributing the suits. Thus we have twelve times the above number, or 136,852,887,600 different arrangements of the cards in a hand giving two of one suit, three of another, and four of each of the two remaining suits. This is of all arrangements the commonest. Out of any large number of hands dealt to any one in a long course of whist-play more than a fifth, or more exactly 342,132,219 out of 1,587,533,899, will be hands containing two four-card suits, a three-card suit and a two-card suit.

Next in frequency come hands containing

one five-card suit, two three-card suits and one two-card suit. Of these there are in all 98,534,079,072, or, roughly, about three hands in twenty are of this kind. Given the suits, which are to have five cards and two cards, there are 8,211,173,256 possible arrangements; but each can be taken twelve different ways by distributing the suits.

The third kind of hand in order of frequency is one containing five of one suit, four of another, three of a third, and one of the fourth. Of such hands there are in all 82,111,732,560; rather more than one hand in eight is of this kind. But when the suits are given to which these several members are to be assigned, we find a very much smaller number of possible arrangements than in the preceding or even than in the next case. For the largeness of the number just mentioned arises from the circumstance that as each suit has a different number of cards, we can distribute the suits in twenty-four instead of twelve different ways (as in each of the last two cases). Thus we can have any one of the four suits for the five-card suit, and combine each of these four with any one of the remaining three suits for the four-card suit, giving twelve combinations, each of which can be combined with two arrangements of the remaining suits as the three-card and one-card suits, giving twenty-four combinations in all. Thus the number of possible arrangements, when the suits are assigned beforehand to the several numbers, is only one twenty-fourth of the number just mentioned, or 3,421,322,190.

The hand coming fourth in order of frequency is one containing one five-card suit, one four-card suit, and two two-card suits. Of such hands there are 67,182,336,640, or about two hands in nineteen are of this kind. But as there are only twelve ways in which the suits can be distributed, we have only to divide this number by twelve instead of by twenty-four, as in the preceding case, to give the number of arrangements when the suits are assigned. We thus get 5,598,527,220 arrangements, a considerably larger number than in the preceding case.

Only fifth in order of frequency comes the hand which many suppose the most frequent, *viz.*, the hand of greatest uniformity of distribution, already considered. The total number of such hands, 66,905,856,160, is very near to the number in the last case; but the number of arrangements when the several suits are assigned is very much greater, being no less than 16,726,464,040.

Here we may stop, noting only that the sixth hand in order of frequency, with a six-card suit, a three-card suit and two two-card suits, comes very far behind the fifth, its number being only 35,830,574,208, or little more than half the number for a four, three, three, three hand. In *How to Play Whist*, the numbers for all possible arrangements of hands are given (p. 196).

But now we should notice that the numbers of ways in which the thirteen cards of a hand may be distributed among the four suits are also the numbers of ways in which the thirteen cards of a suit may be distributed among the four hands. We see, then, that the most probable arrangement is that there will be four cards of the suit in each of two hands, three in another hand, two in the fourth. The next most probable arrangement is that there will be five cards of the suit in one hand, three in each of two other hands, and two in the fourth; and so on, precisely (so far as numerical statistics are concerned) as in the corresponding cases considered above with regard to the distribution of cards in a suit. Only fifth in order of frequency comes the case of what is familiarly called "an honest suit"—that is, a suit which will go round three times. It is more than four and one third times as likely that at least five of a suit will be in one hand (corresponding to the second, third, and fourth cases considered above, and to seven other cases of less frequency, down to the case of eight cards of the suit in one hand and five in another) as that there will not be less than three of the suit in each hand. The chance even that no hand will hold more than four of the suit is less than the chance that there will be five cards in one hand at least. There are about thirteen cases of the former kind to seventeen of the latter.

If any one holds four of a suit, the chance that the suit will go round three times is about

149 to 1,000. But this is not (as has been incorrectly stated of late) the chance that the suit will escape ruffing third round; for that will happen even though the suit does not go around thrice, if partner holds the short suit. A suit, of which the original leader holds four, will escape ruffing by the enemy, if partners hold two, and the adversaries four and three, if partner holds one and the adversaries five and three, or four and four; and lastly, if partner holds none and the adversaries five and four or six and three. The chance is one third in each case that it is partner and not one of the adversaries who holds the short suit.

One other case may be considered. Nearly every one who has played whist much must have had at times a Yarborough hand—that is, a hand in which there is no card above a nine. Pembridge says he has held three of these hands in the course of two hours; but this is, of course, altogether unusual. The name given to a hand of this sort is derived from a certain Lord Yarborough, who used to offer the attractive but really very safe wager of £1,000 to £1, that a hand of this sort would not be dealt. If Lord Yarborough had not calculated the chances (or had them calculated for him) he acted with little wisdom in betting at all on such a matter; but if he knew them he acted with little fairness in offering the odds he did. It will be found that one hand in about 1,828 is a Yarborough, so that Lord Yarborough ought to have wagered £1,827 to £1, instead of £1,000 to £1. It is said that he laid this wager many thousands of times. Supposing he offered £1,000 to £1, to each member of a whist party, for ten deals, on about ninety-one or ninety-two nights, in each of ten years, making in all about 36,560 wagers—*i. e.*, twenty times 1,828—he would have lost about twenty times, or £20,000, and won about £36,500, making a clear profit of about £16,500, or £1,650 per annum, by this seemingly reckless system of wagering.

An instance, lastly, is on record of a hand containing four twos, four threes, four fours and one five. Any one holding such a hand might well believe himself especially selected for punishment by the deities or demons, whoever they may be, who preside over the fortunes of whist-players. Yet such a hand is bound to occur from time to time, when so many play whist. The chance of holding such a hand is, in fact, exactly the same as the chance of holding all the trumps, *viz.*, one in 158,753,389,000. For there are only four possible ways in which such a hand can be made up. It must hold the twelve lowest cards in the pack, and one five, which may be of any of the four suits; hence there are four hands having no card higher than a five out of 635,013,559,600, or one chance of such a hand in 158,753,389,090. Yet I have no manner of doubt—so foolish are men in regard to betting—that if a Lord Yarborough of to-day were to offer £10,000 to £1 (instead of £158,753,389,000 to 1) against the occurrence of such a hand he would find many takers.

R. A. Proctor,
in *Longman's Magazine.*

THE END.

Knickerbocker Nuggets.

NUGGET.—"A diminutive mass of precious metal."

"Little gems of bookmaking."—*Commercial Gazette*, Cincinnati.

"For many a long day nothing has been thought out or worked out so sure to prove entirely pleasing to cultured book-lovers."—*The Bookmaker.*

I.—Gesta Romanorum. Tales of the old monks. Edited by C. SWAN . . . $1 00

"This little gem is a collection of stories composed by the monks of old, who were in the custom of relating them to each other after meals for their mutual amusement and information."—*Williams' Literary Monthly.*

"Nuggets indeed, and charming ones, are these rescued from the mine of old Latin, which would certainly have been lost to many busy readers who can only take what comes to them without delving for hidden treasures."

II.—Headlong Hall and Nightmare Abbey. By THOMAS LOVE PEACOCK . . . $1 00

"It must have been the court librarian of King Oberon who originally ordered the series of quaintly artistic little volumes that Messrs. Putnam are publishing under the name of Knickerbocker Nuggets. There is an elfin dignity in the aspect of these books in their bindings of dark and light blue with golden arabesques."—*Portland Press.*

III.—Gulliver's Travels. By JONATHAN SWIFT. A reprint of the early complete edition. Very fully illustrated. Two vols. $2 50

"Messrs. Putnam have done a substantial service to all readers of English classics by reprinting in two dainty and artistically bound volumes those biting satires of Jonathan Swift, *Gulliver's Travels.*"

IV.—**Tales from Irving.** With illustrations. Two vols. Selected from "The Sketch Book," "Traveller," "Wolfert's Roost," "Bracebridge Hall." $2 00

"The tales, pathetic and thrilling as they are in themselves, are rendered winsome and realistic by the lifelike portraitures which profusely illustrate the volumes. . . . We confess our high appreciation of the superb manner in which the publishers have got up and sent forth the present volumes—which are real treasures, to be prized for their unique character."—*Christian Union.*

"Such books as these will find their popularity confined to no one country, but they must be received with enthusiasm wherever art and literature are recognized."—*Albany Argus.*

V.—**Book of British Ballads.** Edited by S. C. HALL. A fac-simile of the original edition. With illustrations by CRESWICK, GILBERT, and others $1 50

"This is a diminutive fac-simile of the original very valuable edition. . . . The collection is not only the most complete and reliable that has been published, but the volume is beautifully illustrated by skilful artists."—*Pittsburg Chronicle.*

"Probably the best general collection of our ballad literature, in moderate compass, that has yet been made."—*Chicago Dial.*

VI.—**The Travels of Baron Münchausen.** Reprinted from the early, complete edition. Very fully illustrated $1 25

"The venerable Baron Münchausen in his long life has never appeared as well-dressed, so far as we know, as now in this goodly company."

"The Baron's stories are as fascinating as the Arabian Nights."—*Church Union.*

VII.—**Letters, Sentences, and Maxims.** By Lord CHESTERFIELD. With a critical essay by C. A. SAINTE-BEUVE $1 00

"Full of wise things, quaint things, witty and shrewd things, and the maker of this book has put the pick of them all together.—*London World.*"

"Each of the little volumes in this series is a literary gem."—*Christian at Work.*

VIII.—**The Vicar of Wakefield.** By GOLDSMITH. With 32 illustrations by WILLIAM MULREADY $1 00

"Goldsmith's charming tale seems more charming than ever in the dainty dress of the Knickerbocker Nuggets series. These little books are a delight to the eye, and their convenient form and size make them most attractive to all book-lovers."—*The Writer*, Boston.

"A gem of an edition, well made, printed in clear, readable type, illustrated with spirit, and just such a booklet as, when one has it in his pocket, makes all the difference between solitude and loneliness."—*Independent.*

IX.—**Lays of Ancient Rome.** By THOMAS BABINGTON MACAULAY. Illustrated by GEORGE SCHARF $1 00

"The poems included in this collection are too well known to require that attention should be drawn to them, but the beautiful setting which they receive in the dainty cover and fine workmanship of this series makes it a pleasure even to handle the volume."—*Yale Literary Magazine.*

X.—**The Rose and the Ring.** By WILLIAM M. THACKERAY. With the author's illustrations. $1 25

"*The Rose and the Ring*, by Thackeray, is reproduced with quaint illustrations, evidently taken from the author's own handiwork."—*Rochester Post-Express.*

XI.—**Irish Melodies and Songs.** By Thomas Moore. Illustrated by Maclise . . $1 50

"The latest issue is a collection of Thomas Moore's *Irish Melodies and Songs*, fully and excellently illustrated, with each page of the text printed within an outline border of appropriate green tint, embellished with emblems and figures fitting the text."—*Boston Times.*

XII.—**Undine and Sintram.** By De La Motte Fouqué. Illustrated $1 00

"*Undine and Sintram* are the latest issue, bound in one volume. They are of the size classics should be—pocket volumes—and nothing more desirable is to be found among the new editions of old treasures."—*San José Mercury.*

XIII.—**The Essays of Elia.** By Charles Lamb. Two vols. $2 00

"The genial essayist himself could have dreamed of no more beautiful setting than the Putnams have given the *Essays of Elia* by printing them among their Knickerbocker Nuggets."—*Chicago Advance.*

XIV.—**Tales from the Italian Poets.** By Leigh Hunt. Two vols. . . . $2 00

"The perfection of artistic bookmaking."—*San Francisco Chronicle.*

"This work is most delightful literature, which finds a fitting place in this collection, bound in volumes of striking beauty."—*Troy Times.*

"Hunt had just that delightful knowledge of the Italian poets that one would most desire for one's self, together with an exquisite style of his own wherein to make his presentation of them to English readers perfect."—*New York Critic.*

The first series, comprising the foregoing eighteen volumes, in handsome case, $19.00

XV.—Thoughts of the Emperor Marcus Aurelius Antoninus. Translated by GEORGE LONG. $1 00

"The thoughts of the famous Roman are worthy of a new introduction to the army of readers through a volume so dainty and pleasing."—*Intelligencer.*

"As a book for hard study, as a book to inspire reverie, as a book for five minutes or an hour, it is both delightful and profitable."—*Journal of Education.*

"It is an interesting little book, and we feel indebted to the translator for this presentation of his work."—*Presbyterian.*

XVI.—Æsop's Fables. Rendered chiefly from original sources. By Rev. THOMAS JAMES, M.A. With 100 illustrations by JOHN TENNIELL. $1 25

"It is wonderful the hold these parables have had upon the human attention; told to children, and yet of no less interest to men and women."—*Chautauqua Herald.*

"For many a long day nothing has been thought out or worked out so sure to prove entirely pleasing to cultured book-lovers."—*The Bookmaker.*

"These classic studies adorned with morals were never more neatly prepared for the public eye."—*The Milwaukee Wisconsin.*

XVII.—Ancient Spanish Ballads. Historic and Romantic. Translated, with notes, by J. G. LOCKHART. Reprinted from the revised edition of 1841, with 60 illustrations by ALLAN, ROBERTS, SIMSON, WARREN, AUBREY, and HARVEY. $1 50

"A mass of popular poetry which has never yet received the attention to which it is entitled."—*Boston Journal of Education.*

"The historical and artistic settings of these mediæval poetic gems enhance the value and attractiveness of the book."—*Buffalo Chronicle Advocate.*

XVIII.—**The Wit and Wisdom of Sydney Smith.** A selection of the most memorable passages in his Writings and Conversations . $1 00

XIX.—**The Ideals of the Republic;** or, **Great Words from Great Americans.** Comprising: "The Declaration of Independence, 1776"; "The Constitution of the United States, 1779"; "Washington's Circular Letter, 1783," etc. $1 00

XX.—**Selections from Thomas De Quincey.** Comprising: "On Murder Considered as One of the Fine Arts"; Three Memorable Murders"; "The Spanish Nun." $1 00

XXI.—**Tales by Heinrich Zschokke.** Comprising: "A New Year's Eve"; "The Broken Pitcher"; "Jonathan Frock"; "A Walpurgis Night." Translated by PARKE GODWIN and WILLIAM P. PRENTICE $1 00

XXII.—**American War Ballads.** A selection of the more noteworthy of the Ballads and Lyrics which were produced during the Revolution, the War of 1812, the Mexican War, and the Civil War. Edited, with notes, by GEO. CARY EGGLESTON. With original illustrations. Two vols. . $2 50

XXIII.—**The Autobiography of Benjamin Franklin.** Edited, with notes, by JOHN BIGELOW $1 00

XXIV.—**Songs of Fairy Land.** Compiled by EDWARD T. MASON, with illustrations from designs by MAUD HUMPHREY $1 25

XXV.—Sesame and Lilies. By JOHN RUSKIN $1 00

XXVI.—The Garden, as considered in literature by certain polite writers. Edited by WALTER HOWE, with portrait of William Kent . . $1 00

XXVII.—The Boyhood and Youth of Goethe. Comprising the first thirteen books of his Autobiography ("Truth and Poetry from my own Life"). Two vols. $2 00

XXVIII.—The Sayings of Poor Richard. Being the Prefaces, Proverbs, and Poems of Benjamin Franklin, originally printed in Poor Richard's Almanacs for 1733-1758. Collected and Edited by PAUL L. FORD. With portrait of Franklin. $1 00

XXIX.—Love Poems of Three Centuries. Compiled by JESSIE F. O'DONNELL. Two vols. $2 00

XXX.—Chesterfield's Letters. SECOND SERIES. Letters of Philip Dormer, Fourth Earl of Chesterfield, to his Godson and Successor. Now first edited from the originals, with a Memoir of Lord Chesterfield by the Earl of Carnarvon. With portraits and illustrations. Two vols. . $2 00

XXXI.—Representative Irish Stories. Compiled, with Introduction and Notes, by W. B. YEATS. Two vols. $2 00

XXXII.—French Ballads. Printed in the original text. Edited by Prof. T. F. CRANE. Illustrated. $1 50

XXXIII.—Eöthen. Pictures of Eastern Travel. By W. A. KINGLAKE. . . $1 00

XXXIV.—Stories from the Arabian Nights. Selected and edited by STANLEY LANE-POOLE, with additions newly translated from the Arabic. Three volumes. Each volume contains a frontispiece in photogravure and other designs . . $3 00

XXXV.—A Selection from the Discourses of Epictetus; with the Encheiridion. Translated by GEORGE LONG $1 00

XXXVI.—Rasselas, Prince of Abyssinia. By SAMUEL JOHNSON $1 00

XXXVII.—Cranford. By Mrs. GASKELL. $1 00

XXXVIII.—German Ballads. Printed in the original text. Edited by Prof. H. S. WHITE. Illustrated $1 50

G. P. PUTNAM'S SONS, PUBLISHERS
New York and London

www.ingramcontent.com/pod-product-compliance
Lightning Source LLC
Chambersburg PA
CBHW031859220426
43663CB00006B/695